LOVER TO LOVER

LOVER TO LOVER
Secrets of Sex Therapy

Nora Harlow

G. P. Putnam's Sons
New York

The text of this book is set in 11 point Garamond.

Library of Congress Cataloging in Publication Data

Harlow, Nora.
   Lover to lover.

   Includes index.
   1. Sexual intercourse. 2. Sexual disorders.
3. Sex therapy. I. Title.
HQ21.H327   1983   616.85'832   82-25022
ISBN 0-399-12790-9

PRINTED IN THE UNITED STATES OF AMERICA

The sex therapy methods illustrated in *Lover to Lover* are those of:

Gene G. Abel, M.D.
Professor of Clinical Psychiatry
College of Physicians and Surgeons
Columbia University

Director of the Sexual Behavior Clinic
New York State Psychiatric Institute

Past President, Society of Behavioral Medicine

Contents

The Secret World of Sex   11

DESIRE: How to Keep It; What to Do When
It Disappears

The Best of Lovers Three Years Later   17
Her Best Lover □ His Best Times

How Lovers Lose Their Desire   23
*One, Two, Three, Making-a-Baby Sex □ The Most Ig-
nored Fact of Erotic Biology □ The Dangers of Having
"Normal" Sex □ The New-Lover Solution*

Ten Days to Erotic Discovery—Lover to Lover   33
*Relearning the Lover's Body □ Lovers' Time □ Beyond
His Erections to Her Desires □ Lovers' Questions □ Hands-on-Hands Learning □ The Right Touch
for Higher Desire*

Lovemaking as It Was in the Beginning   51
*His Sensitive Spot □ Getting Too High □ Whipped
Cream □ Sex in the Water □ Coming on Her Breasts □
The Testicle High*

The Man Who Lost All Desire for His Wife   55

Five Tricks to Kill Your Desire   63

Five Tricks to Rescue the Lover Who Has Lost
Desire   67

Contents

IMPOTENCE: Doing the Right Things to Get an Erection

Facts About Getting Erections   77
Impotent Men Get Erections □ *Every Man Loses His Erections* □ *The Three Causes of Erection Failure: Biology, Biology, and Biology*

Physical Impotence: What to Do About It   83
The Abel Scale: Six Questions to Help You Decide If You Have Physical Impotence □ *Measuring Your Natural Sleep Erections* □ *Three Vital Steps Before Surgery*

Behavioral Impotence: How It Works   85
Erection Anxiety □ *Profile of the Impotent Man* □ *Every Man Past the Age of Forty*

The First and Easiest Cure Ever for Behavioral Impotence   90

How He Fails to Restore His Erections   93
He Tries to Cure Himself: The Five Worst Mistakes a Man Can Make □ *Choosing the Worst Kind of Lovers*

Doing the Right Things: Five Steps to Getting an Erection   102

Becoming an Excellent Lover Without Using Your Erection   103

Whole Body Touch   104
The Impotent Couple's Usual Reasons for Staying That Way □ *Ten Days to Erotic Discovery—Lover to Lover*

His Lover's Responsibility   107
A Man's Fears He Can't Tell a Woman □ *Touching His Genitals in a Series of Small Steps* □ *Giving Up the Best Orgasm* □ *Breaking the Partial-Erection Habit* □ *The Dangers of Having "Normal" Sex (Reprise)*

Learning to Lose Your Erection in Front of Her   121

How to Stop Trying Harder   122

The Skill of the Lover Assured of Success   125

Contents

HER ORGASM: How to Let Your Lover Help You, Why You May Not Want To, and Why You Should Anyway

Sex Without Trust 128

Facts About Lubricating and Having an Orgasm 133
Lubricating the Natural Way □ Orgasms: Easy, Better, Best

Two Women: The One Who Orgasms and The One Who Doesn't 141

Female Impotence: Distinguishing Between Physical and Behavioral Causes 145

Five Steps to Having an Orgasm With Him 146

How She Fails 147
The Chronically Underaroused Woman's Usual Reasons for Staying That Way □ The No-Responsibility Circle of Failure

Her Body for Her, First 150
She Takes Seven Small Actions to Build Her Arousal □ Reactive Worries □ Vibrators □ Fear of Letting Go □ Finding Out Every Erotic Thing

How She Misses Out on Her Lover's Help 158
What She Likes But Can't Tell Him □ Choosing the Worst Possible Lover

Her Body for the Two of Them: How She Tells Him What She Wants 162
Touching Her More □ About Her Clitoris □ Exploring His Lover's Vagina □ His Body for Her

Her Most Important Sex Act: Trust 172

Contents

OVERCOMING PREMATURE EJACULA-
TION: Secrets of the Man Who Can Last as
Long as He Wants

The Basic Facts of Premature Ejaculation: Why It
Happens; How to Stop It   178
*How a Man Times Ejaculation □ The Moment of Eja-
culatory Inevitability □ Establishing a Biological Pat-
tern □ Making a Man Come Too Fast: Five Causes and
Five Hundred Situations*

The First Cure for Premature Ejaculation   185
*The Four Secrets That Help a Man Last as Long as He
Wants*

The Revised Cure   187
*Dr. Annon's Method □ Dr. Semans's Method □ The
Masters and Johnson Additions*

How He Fails to Succeed   191
*Choosing the Worst Kind of Lover □ He Tries to Cure
Himself: The Five Worst Mistakes a Man Can
Make □ The Circle of Failure*

The First Step to Success: Rejecting Her Rejection   197

He and His Best Lover Follow the Stop-Start System   199

The Pitfalls of Learning to Last   201
*He Comes Too Quickly □ Unrealized Expectations □ The
Sequential-Thinking Handicap □ How She Helps Him*

Two Crises at the Very Last Moment   204
His Penis Stops Working □ He Succumbs to Lust

And He Lasts and Lasts and Lasts   206

Contents

Ten Laws for Lifetime Success   208

Bibliography   211

Index   213

The Secret World of Sex

There is a secret world of sex. It is not at all mysterious. It is only secret.

For me, the discovery that there still were sexual secrets came as a shock. Having grown up as a child of the sexual revolution, I was beyond sex secrets. I knew everything there was to know about sex. Or thought I did. The proof: I knew much more about sex than my mother—and even my father. Which is why I truly believed, like many of the people around me, that there was nothing more to know.

That firm belief was shattered when I became editor of a magazine that advised the nation's one hundred twenty-five thousand physicians on what they could do to help patients with their sex problems. My first days on the job I was astonished to discover that the secrets of overcoming nearly every major sex problem were known.

We do know, it turns out, what causes desire to flourish or die. We do know exactly why men get erections and how all healthy men can teach themselves to get erections—even the ones who are impotent. We know, too, how all men can learn to remain erect as long as they want. We do know techniques to teach sexually shy women how to have orgasms, simple skills that can improve the erotic life of all women. We even know how to protect lovers from ever having problems in the first place. The reports on the erotic body are in. What makes it work. What stops it from working. The secrets of successful sex have been painstakingly

11

discovered and scientifically validated by a handful of specialists. But, to my astonishment, I found that few people used them and most people behaved as though they didn't exist.

As for typhoid fever, the cure for most sexual dissatisfaction was found years ago. And, like typhoid, sexual dissatisfaction should be an extinct condition. Lovers can learn to handle their problems, they can help each other, they can go beyond what they have ever felt erotically. Sex between two people deeply in love is beautiful. Lovers should succeed. But do they?

What continues to astonish is that so many lovers don't. On my desk—along with proof that most sex problems could be cured in a matter of weeks, sometimes in a matter of hours—yet another study which showed that the numbers of lovers reporting trouble with erections, orgasms, and desire were today—despite these known cures—still reported at the exact high levels as the famous Kinsey studies of thirty years ago. In this particular study one hundred married couples were selected, by University of Pittsburgh researcher Dr. Ellen Frank, for the very reason that they were happy in their marriages. Their test scores showed astounding marital success. They loved each other. They were mentally and physically sound people. Every test showed that they were people whose marriages were characterized by each couple's "flexibility, adaptability, ability to confront problems, communicate about them, and work out solutions." So they were sexually happy, right?

Wrong.

These same two hundred people who were so good to their lovers in so many ways were just not very good to their lovers during lovemaking; they showed very little ability to do anything to solve any problem that was sexual. Forty-eight of the women said they had difficulty becoming sexually excited, forty-six said they had difficulty having orgasms, and fifteen said they had never, ever had an orgasm. Thirty-six of the men said they suffered from premature ejaculation and nine said they had difficulty maintaining an erection. The complaints went on: sixteen men and thirty-five women said they were unable to relax and, sadly, thirty-eight women and twenty-one men said, as far as sex went, they were just not interested. A cure had been found but the patient was still sick.

Except for the few couples who take part in sex therapy, our culture has been unaffected by the cure. Few men report that they do anything consciously to maintain healthy erections or last longer, few women report that they have taught their lovers to help them come easily to orgasm, and practically no lover, man or woman, is able to list the things one should do to keep desire high through the ups and downs of a long relationship.

The cures are known, but the culture goes on, seemingly oblivious for the most part. While the media reflect the latest progress in other areas of bodily function, advances in erotic knowledge remain unnoticed.

Sex book authors still advise lovers to "communicate" but don't tell them what it is they are to communicate. And some of these authors still suggest that impotence is hopeless or that one can and perhaps should solve one's problems with a lover by oneself. These authors still argue over the exact numbers of men and women who have problems (and what kinds of problems) and fail to mention that healthy lovers need never have any problems in the first place or that those who do could overcome the problems with only the help of their lovers—if they knew the secrets of sex therapy.

To help me come to a very personal understanding of how those secrets can change the lives of lovers, I asked my husband, a physician who is also a sex therapist and sex researcher, to train me to be his co-therapist. I saw the lovers' tears, heard their feelings of hopelessness. And I saw them change. Couples who started out sitting angrily apart would appear for the third hour of therapy smiling at each other, sitting close, holding hands. To their great surprise, a few hours of doing the right things in bed seemed to have given them miraculous cures.

Sex therapy clearly worked. My next question: Were couples who sought therapy vastly different from all the rest of the lovers?

To find out about the secret sex lives of ordinary lovers, I talked to them—to the woman alone, to the man alone, to the lovers together, and I discovered that, like the seriously troubled lovers, many, many of these lovers had the same anxieties, were troubled by the same difficulties, and in all cases they kept these feelings secret, especially from the only source of help—their lovers.

Having agreed to tell me everything about their sex lives on the condition that they be unrecognizable to "the neighbors down the block . . . our parents . . . our children," the lovers talked for hundreds of hours. The transcripts—time after time—repeat four identical concerns: the wish to feel more desire, the wish to get more erections more readily, the wish to keep erections as long as he wants, and the wish that she come easily to orgasm. All are wishes easily granted by the lovers themselves in the privacy of their own bedrooms. *If* the lovers know the secrets of sex therapy. So I decided to make the secrets readily available for all lovers to use—lovers with problems and lovers who want never to have problems. And I decided further that the best way to reveal these secrets of erotic success was in the lovers' own words. Who better to tell the story of how to use our new erotic knowledge than the successful lovers themselves?

Accordingly, all the incidents described in this book actually happened. They happened not once to one person but again and again to many people. The words spoken by the lovers are the real words of real lovers. Names have been changed, of course, and a few of the lovers are composites, four to ten real people combined to illustrate all the peculiarities of a particular sex problem.

Real lovers actually changing their erotic behavior are a bit different from the lovers pictured in many books; they have strong emotions and a history of hurt which makes them wary. Being human, even when they know what they should do, they sometimes balk. They are often anxious. They have real-life lovers who are difficult. And they need to know more than what to do. They need to know why each step is necessary, what they can expect to feel as they change their erotic behavior, why their lovers may be reluctant to help them—*and* what to do then.

In their own words, they tell us how to use this new knowledge. They describe their sex problems, tell what they have done with a therapist to correct the problem, what they feel about themselves and their lovers, and what they actually do alone—lover to lover.

DESIRE
How to Keep It; What to Do When It Disappears

The Best of Lovers Three
Years Later

Her Best Lover

*He knew I wanted to feel his tongue inside me . . . First he did that. . . .
Well . . . first he washed my face with a warm cloth. I find this real deli-
cious. Mouth and hands on my breasts. A basin of hot water near the bed
. . . warm wet toweling against my skin. He washed my feet, licked around
my toes, sucked my toes, moved his hands up the inside of my legs. I remember his tongue on my thigh. He licked my thighs real slow while his fingers
rolled through the ringlets around my clit . . . slide . . . slide . . . and then
I said, "Now." He put his penis in . . . right then. I held onto the spokes in
the headboard. He ran his hands from my wrists down to my armpits,
while he thrusted harder and harder. I told him, "Shallow." Shallow
thrusts feel best for me. I held the base of his penis. He said, "More," when
he wanted me to hold tighter. I did. Our sex together was . . . we were one
sexual being . . . fulfilling . . . beyond ourselves. It was like a drug. A
perfect high.*

17

His Best Times

> *She was wonderfully wet and warm. Her tongue under mine. She put the warm towel around my testicles, ran it back and around my anus. I licked my way up her body—up higher on her thighs . . . and higher . . . turned to the side so she could reach my cock. She held it in her warm wet hands . . . slid around while I slid my tongue over her clit . . . slick. She knew I liked her to use both hands and to hold tighter and tighter as we built. I wouldn't put it in unless she told me she really wanted it. I stopped and told her she had to wait. I told her she wasn't ready. She drove me wild. I came so hard I thought I was going to die.*

Sara and Barry were best of friends first and then best of lovers. That was one of the reasons they got married: the sex was *so* good. It's been three years since their passion for each other was an obsession. A lot has happened since then. They left college, they married, the two of them took over his father's bakery and doubled the profits. They bought a new house. Sara and Barry are proud of having built so much together. Unfortunately, in those three years they lost something—their burning desire to enjoy each other's body.

In separate interviews they described what they did last night in bed. The lovemaking they once described as a perfect "high" and an experience so intense he thought he was "going to die" has become "the usual."

> *I just reached over and started feeling her ass. That's how I let her know I want to have intercourse. Sara has a great ass. From the day I met her I've wanted to move my fingers around on her ass. I felt around her vagina a little till I got an erection.*

> *He sort of tweaked my nipple, which I find irritating, so I always lean up against him when he does that so he has to stop. I like my breasts in his mouth, he pulls real strong. He did that for about thirty seconds. And he knows that I like it, but he stopped. . . . Sex feels . . . lately . . . like hard work. I don't know . . . I lately . . . I separate myself from my body. . . . He puts his hands on me. I feel his hands, but I'm not really there. I'm separate, far away somewhere. I'm totally gone.*

18

Desire

I really had a nice stiff hard-on. And she didn't say anything so I fig-ured it was okay to screw. She could see that I was really getting excited . . . that she was really making me hot. She was real quiet, but women are like that during sex.

I like the feeling of his penis going into my vagina. I feel generalized warm feelings . . . I almost never get the real high anymore . . . that I get when I use my own hand. My thoughts kept drifting off . . . I had to get things for dinner . . . green noodles . . . to the dry cleaner . . . I saw him driving his dirty clothes away in his car . . . I could feel his body real heavy on me . . . in and out . . . boring.

I kind of spread her legs pretty fast and I thrusted hard. I think she liked that. That's always the best for me. I was flashing on this broad that comes into the bakery . . . those shiny skinlike pants, and, I swear, you can see each crease, each individual pubic hair, she's all little curly hairs and ridges . . . and she leans over . . . real turned on. I can see her big brown breasts right past her creamy brown nipples . . . and I'm thinking, Where is the white from her bathing suit?

I tried to get back into it. I fantasized him licking my thighs . . . him wrapping me in warm wet towels . . . pulling me toward him by a beauti-ful gold chain around my waist. . . .

I really pumped away. Which kept my cock up, but when I tried to slow down, I was losing it. That's the bitch, if I slow down. I got back into it by biting her shoulder. She yelled and . . . that's the only way we seem to con-nect lately. She was using her hand like she usually does. Feeling my cock in her and all of that was probably turning her on.

I was working on it . . . he was thrusting and pushing . . . and he came . . . and I was sort of relieved. Usually, I come before him. . . . But I could see I wasn't going to have an orgasm, and after a while I got real tired of trying.

She was real quiet so I just kept thrusting like crazy. I came in about five minutes.

19

The "usual" leaves the lovers with feelings of loss. The passion that brought them together and that they thought, because they were so much in love, would last forever is gone.

Barry is surprised and philosophical:

> I always thought we'd keep making love in that great way forever. When you come to think about it, it's bound to happen. There is no way sex can be exciting. I mean it was great but then we did it a hundred times.

Sara is sad:

> I guess you can't make someone go on wanting you. That's what hurts so much. When we make love ... he's stopped touching me like he really loves me. I can't stand not being loved.

Speaking privately, each lover worries about how much the other lover knows.

Barry:

> She knows. She knows I don't want her that much. I think she must know. She's stopped talking about having kids. And having a baby is a very big emotional deal to her.
>
> I love Sara, I'll always love her. And there is no use lying. Well, I like to get off, but it's working-hard sex. It's "getting off" sex. Hollow.
>
> What can I tell you, we've been through things together. Real difficult stuff. I'm used to sticking by Sara, so I'm sticking. If we end up going through life as just companions, without the sex, what can I tell you, I love Sara.

Sara:

> I'm never going to tell him that he bores me in bed. I can't say something real mean like that. He knows I love him. If I tell him that physical sex with him gets me as excited as ironing clothes, I'd be rejecting Barry where he is completely vulnerable ... totally helpless.

Wrong thought.
Barry is far from helpless. So is she.

But Sara is certain. Desire, she believes, happens beyond the lover's control. It is mysterious. And once you lose it there is no hope. As Sara speaks, her eyes fill with tears. She looks far past her present world.

> The warm cloths . . . the long nights of feeling him so intensely. That's what hurts so much. The best lover I ever had . . . and the worst . . . same man. I've still got the man, but the feeling between Barry and me . . . it's almost gone. I love him. And I want to feel passion, but I feel almost nothing.

Love without passion. That should never exist. If Sara and Barry love each other but feel no passion, the two of them are doing something wrong.

The human body is designed to enjoy passionate erotic sex. Lovers should feel passion—*always*. Desire loss linked to being long-time lovers is the most common of all sex problems and the easiest to correct. Lovers in love, no matter how long they've been together, can easily feel passion again. And they should.

Barry and Sara say they want to make love as they did in the beginning. Secretly they believe if they loved each other "enough" they would feel desire.

Wrong belief.

They got into this trouble in the first place the way most couples do—*because* they cared for each other. They loved each other so much they decided to stay together.

Staying together changes the lovers' lovemaking. The commitment to one person demands that the lovers go beyond the easy passion of early eroticism—or else they lose desire. It is easy enough to learn how to go beyond early eroticism. Unfortunately, the fact that there is an additional erotic skill that they have yet to learn is a secret no one has ever told them.

Sara and Barry believe that it is their desire that makes them want to make love in an exciting way and to try new erotic acts. They believe they've lost the desire and *therefore* they can no longer be erotic with a long-time lover. The opposite is true. They stopped *doing* the erotic acts they liked, stopped discovering their new erotic desires, stopped giving each other pleasure and, as they stopped, their desire died.

No matter.

Their desire will come back by itself if they behave the way lovers who feel passion always behave. Which will be particularly easy for Barry and Sara because they've done it once and nearly gotten it perfect.

Barry says, "That's the real killer. We did ... we do ... everything right." Time went by, that's all, says Sara. A mean trick of the gods to snatch away passion. Actually there was no snatching away. They did it themselves. It all happened quite innocently: Barry and Sara killed their desire in a systematic manner by doing what most couples do: They did it right and then they tried to hold on to the one true sex act.

What they did right:

- They loved each other.
- They lusted for each other.
- The *reason* they got together was that they found in each other the person with whom they most wanted to do every possible sexual thing.
- They chose the erotic acts—selected all the things they wanted to do. They got it just right.
- And they liked the way they had sex so much that they did it again. And again. And every time was great.
- And then they said proudly to themselves—hold it right there— we've got it perfect.

The fatal flaw: *repetition destroys desire.*

It has to, because erotic sex is alive. Erotic sex happens *between* two living bodies. Repeat the perfect sex act and it dies.

Barry and Sara made a colossal error. They discovered all the new and wonderful erotic acts they loved. And then, as if they thought they were two highly skilled workers who had mastered the intricacies of building a Rolls-Royce, they planned to keep rolling similar sex acts off the assembly line the rest of their lives. They had the answer. They thought. But did they?

He ran his hands from my wrists down to my armpits while he thrusted harder and harder. . . . Shallow thrusts feel best . . .

By the tenth time, the feel of his hand running *from my wrists down to my armpits* bored Sara because her body is human. Mastery of her body is quite different from mastery of an inanimate object.

Bodies change. Sara's body changes so much that the erotic touch she loved when they were first discovering each other's body is much less erotic to her present body.

Unfortunately, Barry believes Sara's body is as unchangeable as a rock.

> The real trouble . . . well, the trouble is . . . we know everything about each other. When you come to think of it—that's it . . . old bodies too used to each other.
>
> I swear, Sunday morning she walked through the bedroom and I didn't *notice* that she was naked. I've told her to wear her clothes— she walks around naked so much it kills the mystery . . . it's getting like we're brother and sister.

An illusion. What Barry thinks he sees—the same old Sara in the same old body—is a mirage. Sara walking naked through the bedroom is no longer inhabiting the same naked body he's made love to hundreds of times. Touching Sara's body in ways that drove her wild two years ago is a mistake. That's the problem: he makes love to the old body that he knew so well two years ago. Wrong body. Sara lives in a new body.

No matter how exciting the lovemaking, if it stays the same, the animal body will eventually get enough. Sara's body satiates. And then, her body rebels. So does her lover's. They lose desire for the old touch. Nobody's fault.

How Lovers Lose Their Desire

Not only does the erotic body demand change, the erotic body demands *more change than most lovers can imagine.*

Lovers need:
New Bodies
New Touch

New Surroundings
New Thoughts

All Barry and Sara have to do is fulfill those needs. Which is why the passion of early eroticism is so easy. When Barry and Sara were at the height of their passion for each other, they believed the passion came "naturally." Not quite. The lovers' passion came at the beginning because they fulfilled their need for new erotic experiences.

New Bodies

Barry:
   I imagined her without her clothes. I spent a lot of time doing that, and she looked like I had imagined ... except better ... real alive skin, nipples ... way out ... and she has a tattoo ... a rosebud on her ass ... I *loved* it.

New Touch

Finding out everything about her body was Barry's new hobby. Asked what he did for exercise, Barry said, "Screw my brains out."

Sara:
   I used to [*she whispers*] go down on him, but ... that's when we were ... before we were married ... *everything* made me excited then.

New Thoughts

Sara:
   Well, I was feeling powerful ... oh, goodness, I had thoughts: This is going to get him [*giggles*] and it probably did.

New Surroundings

Sara:
   I was so into sex and into Barry. It makes me feel a little embarrassed now, but I would come out of class—for goodness sake—in my raincoat with no underpants. We'd hit Motel Row—and just

go into the first crummy place, pull down the blinds, shut the door, and just go on. Sometimes we'd have sex in the car or his friend's empty house. All we cared about was sex. There was nothing else in the world. Sometimes I couldn't remember whether it was day or night.

In the beginning the lovers fulfilled these basic needs in the easiest possible way. It was so simple when their every erotic act *was new*.

Unfortunately, Barry and Sara fail to make this distinction. Without knowing the real reasons they lost desire, they do what people have always done—they make up a story to explain it.

Barry's stories:

- When you come to think of it, she isn't that interested in me and that gets communicated. Who wants to make love to someone who is only half there?
- It's her body. I look at her body and I don't get that big wallop I used to get.
- It's natural. You read any book on the subject. All the experts say passion just gets less after the honeymoon—I mean, it makes sense. There's all that excitement about getting it and then you've got it. The experts are telling me to look for "deeper meaning in the relationship," but hell, they don't fool me—that's just another way of saying the real good sex times are over.

Sara's stories:

- He excites me sometimes, he just doesn't excite me like he used to.
- The sophisticates say you never get *married* for sex, sex is always better outside of marriage.
- I can't help myself if I don't *want* to put out a lot of effort for him in bed.
- It's natural to lose desire; you can't go panting after each other like teenagers your whole life.
- It's the way he makes love. He's the kind of man who just isn't sensitive to a woman's body.
- Sex isn't that important. There are more important things in a relationship.

• Sex isn't that important, and nothing can be done about it anyway.

The payoff: The stories take the lovers off the hook. Sara tells herself that it is *not* that she is an inadequate lover because she has stopped fulfilling Barry's erotic needs. No, she tells herself: "I have lost desire." The condition—loss of desire—relieves her of any responsibility for creating an erotic life beyond early love.

Which is not necessarily her fault or Barry's. They did the right things naturally at the start. At first, making love was easy. All they had to do was be spontaneous. But after a few years, doing the right things to build desire no longer occurs spontaneously. This is a shock to most lovers. And like most lovers, Sara and Barry meet this experience innocently. They have no idea there is something more to learn about sex. Their idea of sex is a simple one frozen into their minds as children: sex is making a baby.

One, Two, Three, Making-a-Baby Sex

Asked if she knows the facts of erotic biology, Sara says she knows *everything*.

> Really. I know everything there is to know about sex. I had sex education. Mrs. Mendenhall taught our freshman class everything. I think she felt like gagging every time she said the word "penis," but she said it. We got it all ... penis, testicles, ripening eggs, menstruation, the seven stages of the developing fetus, sperm with tails ... you name it, we got it.

Sara has learned how to reproduce; she has learned only a little about how to be erotic. This confuses her.

Reproductive biology and erotic biology are separate entities. The term "having sex" unfortunately has come to mean putting the penis in the vagina, thrusting, and ejaculating. Like many couples, Barry and Sara after the first months of eroticism have begun to rivet their attention wholly on the reproductive aspect of their sexuality. Which puts the lovers in the position of rushing past their need to generate desire—so that they are immediately into what they've been taught is the sex part: erection and ejaculation.

Ironic. Sara is *terrified* of getting pregnant:

> I have an IUD and I make Barry wear a condom. I got pregnant my junior year in college. I was using a diaphragm and it was real close to the end of my period—like the next day. Totally unbeliev-able happening. Everybody was after me to *do* something—to get an abortion. I was real confused. But something inside me just froze. I had the baby—went to classes, no wedding ring, getting bigger and bigger, and, weird, I met Barry. First, he was my friend. We were both business majors and he told me about his dad's bak-ery, and I had all these ideas, which gave him ideas. We kept talk-ing even at the hospital. That saved my life. Having something else to focus on . . . besides my baby . . . my little boy, the one I gave up for adoption.
>
> When I have my real baby it's going to be so planned and so special. A real wanted baby.
>
> When we're ready—really ready—we'll have a baby. I want a baby. But this time it's going to be totally right. A totally wanted baby with parents who will stay together forever.

Barry and Sara go to great lengths to stop themselves from reproduc-ing. Yet, like many couples, they make love as though their only goal is reproduction. Barry approaches Sara as though his life depended on doing everything possible to get her pregnant. He must get an erection immediately, penetrate, ejaculate, and get that sperm flowing toward that egg.

Like most couples, Sara and Barry have never learned to be erotic. Which brings us to—

The Most Ignored Fact of Erotic Biology

Erections, lubrication, and orgasm follow *what lovers* do *to arouse each other.*

Everybody's body works the same way. First the erotic touch—the right touch—and then, without the lovers' doing anything at all, they get erections, they lubricate, they have orgasms. Biological law: if you teach your lover to give you the touch you most desire and your lover gives you what you want—all the rest follows naturally.

If all Barry and Sara ever learned about sexual biology in their whole lives was that one fact, they could do very well as lovers. That is, if they truly understood its importance. And if they acted in bed in a way that showed they believed the fact was true.

> *I like my breasts in his mouth, he pulls real strong. He did that for about thirty seconds. And he knows that I like it, but he stopped. . . .*

When Barry licks Sara's breasts, they both become aroused—and that arousal triggers the autonomic nervous system to automatically send their blood rushing about their bodies. When he stops before she wants him to, her arousal drops.

Notice, it is their automatic systems that send their blood rushing about their bodies—not Barry or Sara. Erections and lubrication are reflex actions. Beyond their control. Like a knee jerk. And so is orgasm.

Arousing each other is what Barry and Sara do. Reflex is what their bodies do. Their arousal sustains their erections and lubrication. Barry and Sara have sex without giving that biological fact much thought. As their relationship continues they skip the arousal part—the part they do control—and go directly for the reflex.

Barry:
> *I really pumped away. Which kept my cock up, but when I tried to slow down, I was losing it. That's the bitch.*

Sara:
> *. . . I was working on it . . . and he came . . . and I was sort of relieved.*

If erections and orgasms are reflexes out of the lovers' control, why do lovers think so much about erections and orgasms?

The answer is biology. Barry and Sara, being part of an animal species—a higher species of animal to be sure—have a biological drive to reproduce. Like all animals, Barry and Sara may carry an innate genetic trait that helps them do that one sex act instinctually. Reproductive sex is what Barry and Sara do naturally. Erotic sex is what they have to learn.

And what is the biggest obstacle to their learning?

Penis-in-the-vagina intercourse.

The Dangers of Having "Normal" Sex

The animal drive to reproduce is strong. It goes on regardless of the lovers' desire to have a baby. To help lovers forget about the phenomenal number of erotic delights they might enjoy and to keep them focused on reproducing the race, nature throws in a great incentive: orgasm.

At first Barry and Sara touched each other many different ways. And then *they had an orgasm following penis-in-the-vagina intercourse.* Barry and Sara *loved* their first orgasm together. So they had another one. And another one. And another one. *Before* each orgasm his penis was in her vagina. Orgasm is a powerful reinforcer. Whatever Barry and Sara do immediately *before* orgasm they have an animal urge to do again. And they do. They get into the habit of doing it fairly well. And before they know it, they have stopped doing a great many erotic acts in favor of concentrating on the reproductive essentials. Like most long-time lovers, their lovemaking becomes stylized. A couple of kisses, a bit of breast play, penetrate, thrust, and have an orgasm.

This new shorter erotic experience feels great. Which leads lovers to rush off happily in the wrong direction.

Barry found that he and Sara needed to do less and less to get erotically excited *before* orgasm. He loved it. So did Sara. Rather than acknowledging the biological forces behind the rush to orgasm, they mistakenly believed this was happening because they—being completely different from so many of their sexually bored friends—were great lovers.

Barry:

My god, to be with a woman who wanted to get right down to it—I loved it. And, *she* loved it. That's what was so great. She wanted me to get right to her. She was so hot. She couldn't wait. This was the woman I'd dreamed about, ready to come the second I touched her.

And, consequently, Barry touched her in fewer and fewer new ways. The repetitive act of penis-in-the-vagina intercourse assured the orgasm. But it was destined to kill the desire.

What was so wonderful for a while led to great disappointment.

Barry:

> From the outside, people . . . well, guys look at Sara. I see them. They're jealous. They'd give anything to get into bed with her. Hell, that was at least half the excitement for me. I wanted to get to her before some other guy did. Off with her clothes and right into her. I'm still interested. I'm just not *that* interested.

Sara:

> I have an orgasm, but sometimes I feel what is the use of Barry even being there? I might as well be by myself . . . I swear it's no different than jerking off. So why bother?

At the point where they find themselves having "just sex," lovers have two options:

1. Go in search of a new lover.
2. Stay and search—lover to lover—for the passion that lies beyond the boundaries of early eroticism.

Unfortunately, neither Barry nor Sara knows about this second option. They both believe that each man and woman together come to a way of making love which is uniquely theirs—as personal and unchangeable as their fingerprints. They believe they've completely developed the way they make love. And it's unsatisfactory.

They believe they're stuck. They believe they have to touch each other in the same unsatisfying way forever. Faced with that option, neither lover is extremely eager to have sex.

Unfortunately, as most lovers do, Barry and Sara fail to make the most vital distinction: *the lover's behavior is separate from the lover.* They believe they have lost desire for the part of their lover that can never change— the lover's very body and the lover's very being. A diabolically painful mistake.

The vital distinction: *lovers lose desire for their lover's behavior.*

Even though they loved each other so much they signed the marriage papers, their first inclination is to solve this problem in the way they have in the past, in the usual way one solves one's dating problems—date somebody else.

The New-Lover Solution

Barry dreams of his past lovers:

> I had . . . so many girls . . . more than Sara suspects . . . well, with Sara . . . it was magic.

And, while he's thinking about his old girlfriends, Sara meets someone new.

> I have a lover . . . I mean besides Barry. . . . The word *lover* sounds funny. I didn't think . . . we'd actually really do it . . . just playing around . . . flirting . . . teasing . . . he'd call me Mrs. Smith, a lot of emphasis on the "Mrs." I thought it was love 'cause I enjoyed the sex so much. And I liked the sex 'cause . . . well, I was flattered. . . . I've always felt a little insecure . . . I've never been sure that I could really arouse a man . . . and Barry . . . the changes we've been through with sex . . . made me feel real rejected.
>
> I had some fantasies about leaving Barry for this guy. Just fantasies. I was feeling Barry didn't love me anymore. He had just bought me this beautiful house—a home for the two of us—so I *knew* he did love me, but without the feeling that he wanted me in bed, I felt totally rejected.

Finding a new lover does work. Which tends to confuse all of us. Barry can't compete with Sara's new lover because her new lover *knows* he is with a new body—a body whose eroticism he must discover—and so they select the new touch they want at that moment. They are in new erotic surroundings and think new erotic thoughts. And, by the laws of the erotic biology of desire, what must happen happens—Sara's desire level shoots up.

Making love to a new lover *is* better for Sara because the new lover won't let Sara stay the same. He makes her reveal what she likes. And because she is letting her lover know what erotic acts she finds enjoyable right at the moment she feels more desire.

The catch. The joys of early eroticism last only until:

- He stops touching her as though she has a new body.
- She stops selecting the exact touch she wants.
- They stop changing the surroundings.
- They stop thinking new erotic thoughts.

As Sara discovers, it isn't finding *the* lover that makes the difference—making love to any new lover works beautifully to regenerate desire as long as he *is* a new lover.

Sara found out the painful truth about the new-lover situation:
It isn't as though I can find another man and go through life having great sex with him while I build a great marriage with my husband. This guy isn't going to be the lover, he's going to be the *first* lover, and then I'll have to find a new guy after that and . . . on like that.

Irony. Barry and Sara yearn for new bodies—the touch between new bodies—and yet they have that, even if they stay together forever. The challenge: *to discover the new body of the familiar lover.*

Most lovers would never think of going to a sex therapist for common boredom, but Sara, feeling herself drifting farther and farther from Barry toward separation and divorce, is determined to get the best advice.

The sex therapist suggests they touch each other in ways they find more pleasurable.

Barry says:
We do that. We like to fuck. And we do. It's getting boring.

What Barry wants is to rejuvenate his desire by making love just the way he usually does—the natural way, being spontaneous. Logically that is impossible. Spontaneously, Barry has the animal urge to penetrate, thrust, and come. And that is the one sex act he and Sara do perfectly. What they need is help rebuilding their desire.

What Barry and Sara need is a structure that will help them to discover the erotic acts that they find uniquely pleasurable. The best structure is one developed by sex therapists, the one that has helped thousands of couples far more seriously troubled than Barry and Sara. The Lover's Plan—Ten Days to Erotic Discovery, helps lovers go beyond the joys of early eroticism to discover a forever way of making love.

Ten Days to Erotic Discovery—
Lover to Lover

Basic instructions to be followed on all ten days: To discover which touch is most erotic, touch one part of your lover's body. Wash her arms. Dry her arms. Give her choices. For half an hour. Your lover is to do the same for you on alternate days.

Day 1: Touch your lover's arms and hands.
Day 2: Your lover touches your arms and hands.
Day 3: Touch your lover's legs and feet.
Day 4: Your lover touches your legs and feet.
Day 5: Touch your lover's head and body (excluding genitals).
Day 6: Your lover touches your head and body (excluding genitals).
Day 7: Touch your lover's genitals.
Day 8: Your lover touches your genitals.
Day 9: Discover which touch, positions, and movements your lover finds most erotic during penis-in-the-vagina intercourse.
Day 10: Your lover discovers which touch you find most erotic during penis-in-the-vagina intercourse.

During the ten days of erotic discovery
Find out:

• How your lover would like to be touched. With fingers? With whole hand? With two hands? With tongue? What combinations of touch? How much pressure? Soft? Rough? How her preferences change at different levels of arousal.
• When your lover wants to be touched.

- With what accessories your lover would like to be caressed. In water? With oil? With perfumed soap? What smell? With music? On a fur rug?

Your role: Take care of your lover completely.
The goal: Decide which touch is better.
Your lover's role: Build a list of the erotic pleasures that you can share—lover to lover.
Time: Half an hour. Every day for ten days.

During the ten days of erotic discovery
Do:
- Give your lover many, many sensual options from which to choose.
- Continue touching for the full half hour.

Don't:
- Have penis-in-the-vagina intercourse or orgasm before Days Nine and Ten. If you want to have penis-in-the-vagina intercourse or an orgasm, separate that experience from the experience of relearning your lover's body.
- Caress your lover during your time to be caressed. You must use all your concentration to discover your eroticism. Only that for half an hour.

Why does the ten-day plan work? The plan works—has worked for thousands of couples—and will always work because the Ten-Day Plan:

- Gives lovers immediate physical pleasure.
- Slows down the sexual experience so that each lover has time to feel each separate touch and to *discriminate* which erotic touches are better.
- Gives each lover complete responsibility for making the other feel good; gives each lover the freedom to be erotically pleased.
- Brings lovers closer together doing an erotic act at which they cannot fail.
- Takes the lovers' focus away from the genital area, relieving them of the assumption that they know everything, relieving them of high emotions and dissatisfaction they may feel about their previous experiences and jolting them into a new erotic experience whose lessons can later be applied to genital caress.

· Gives couples a structure which allows them to discover what touch they find erotically pleasurable without the pressures and distractions of penis-in-the-vagina intercourse.

Relearning the Lover's Body

Day 1: He Touches His Lover's Arms

A simple task. Find out exactly what erotic touch she wants now. Wash her arms, dry her arms, stroke her arms. Offer her choices of water temperature, soap, smells, oils. Give her everything she wants for half an hour.

Barry thinks he has heard incorrectly:
Okay. We touch each other's arms. Right?

Wrong. To discover what Sara finds more pleasurable, Barry is to touch her. Only. She is to decide which of the many variations is better. That's the first change. They no longer touch each other at the same time.

I started feeling her ass. I felt around her vagina a little.

He sort of tweaked my nipple . . . my breasts in his mouth for about thirty seconds. . . . I like the feeling of his penis. . . .

Far too much going on for Sara to be able to sort out exactly which touch she wants more of. To discover which erotic touch she likes better, she needs the one-way erotic experience—and so does Barry.

Barry:
I cannot imagine what there is about Sara's arms that I could possibly spend half an hour finding out. It makes me feel dumb . . . What happens if we finish before the half hour?

Good question. Impossible to "finish" before the half hour because the rule is: *Continue for half an hour.*

35

Barry:
>   But that wouldn't be spontaneous.

Right again. Spontaneously, they have made love until their sexual interest in each other has nearly died. To change means doing new sexual activities—activities that—because they are new—will feel unfamiliar, perhaps even uncomfortable.

Lovers' Time

Going slow is a drastic change. What Barry and Sara feel most comfortable doing is staying the same.

>   *... I just reached over and started feeling her ass.... I came ... I guess ... in about five minutes.*

Staying the same means having a *very* short erotic experience:

- From first sexual touch to last in less than ten minutes.
- Less than ten minutes of erotic sex a week.
- Less than half an hour of erotic sex in a month.

The Ten-Day Plan jolts the lovers into a new time frame: half an hour. Which is enough of an initial change for lovers with a past history of short quick sex. Enthusiastic, happy lovers may enjoy taking longer.

Barry:
>   I touched the skin on her arms and hands—every square inch. Over and finished in eight minutes. A *long* eight minutes.

And, *voilà,* Barry has done what most lovers do as they try to change, he has duplicated the *pattern* of his weekly lovemaking.

The Problem: Barry, left to his own devices, has no way of knowing how to go slow.

Vague instructions to take one's time—advice often given to lovers— is not enough. Asked to discover which kinds of erotic touch pleases his lover, from her armpits to the tips of her fingers—with no further guidelines—Barry finds out everything in his usual few minutes and concludes, "Oh yeah, I did that, I slowed down—didn't work." The rule: Continue for half an hour. Barry does—*after* he gets by his greatest obstacles.

Beyond His Erections to Her Desires

Barry:

It felt all right . . . well, what can I say, I didn't get excited or get an erection or anything and I think I'm like a lot of guys. I mean, her arms are soft and touching her is okay . . . but touching her arms doesn't really excite me.

Wrong goal: He is to *discover* which of many touches excites *her*. And he does it again. He duplicates his lovemaking pattern: Barry touches Sara's arms just as he touches her genitals during penis-in-the-vagina intercourse.

I felt around her vagina a little till I got an erection.

Barry touches Sara to make Barry feel good, to help Barry get an erection. Which is to be expected considering his past experience. Being human, Barry experiences his own bodily feelings intensely. He feels most erotic with his erect penis thrusting into Sara's vagina. Being overwhelmed by these feelings he tries—instinctually—to duplicate them. Being an intelligent fellow, he knows Sara's feelings in her body are different, but he never *feels* them. Her bodily feelings are an abstract concept. So hard for Barry or Sara or any lover to go beyond their own intense bodily feeling to discover—that great abstraction—the lover's eroticism.

Unfortunately, before Barry can learn what Sara wants he has to give up his natural obsession with his own intense sexuality. Temporarily, he needs to move past the notion that his first erotic need is to get an erection.

Fact: Barry has gotten many erections in his life and he will get many more, and not one past, present, or future erection will give him any information about how to touch his lover in ways that make her feel erotic. In fact, *his* erection has nothing to do with it.

Back to the goal: Touch Sara to make Sara feel good. How? Ask her what she wants and give it to her.

Change is difficult. Barry struggles along feeling uncomfortable—but no matter. He and Sara do what is important. They change.

- They experience erotic touch for half an hour.
- He discovers some new erotic pleasures she likes.
- He begins a list of ways to please Sara.

Given the time and her lover's complete attention, Sara reveals secrets. Barry discovers that Sara wants him to

—Touch her new body in new ways:

> She likes me to touch her upper arms ... more than I would think ... a light touch ... repetitious ... she wants to feel the warmth of the rough skin ... calluses on my palms. She likes oil ... for me to slide my oily fingers along the inside of her fingers ... my fingertips over the palms of her hands ... slower and slower. She likes to feel my tongue in the palm of her hand.
>
> The one thing that drove her wild ... she wants me to kiss her underarms and lick them ... we saw this picture of a guy doing this in a sex book and I said, "Yech." 'Cause I hate any touch under my arms so she thought I wouldn't do it ... do it to her ... but I like to feel her so sexy. I was licking her real slow and she was rolling around. . . .

—In new surroundings:

> She wants to have sex in the daylight with the shades down. The phone has to be off the hook. And I ... she bought some ... she likes me to wear boxer shorts.

—Which generates new thoughts:

> I was thinking on the way to work, what I wanted him to do next.

Desire

Day 2: She Touches His Arms

Sara slows her lover down. She oils his hands, touches slow and light, the back of his hands, each finger, his forearm, elbow, inside of his upper arm. And she finds out two things: he likes his palms touched; he finds her lace panties provocative. Time: fifteen minutes.

Sara:

> I've always felt real insecure . . . I always worried about whether I could really arouse a man.
>
> I guess I'm just clumsy. I don't know what men want. I don't read sex books. Besides I don't believe in doing sex like a paint-by-the-numbers kit. Mechanical sex doesn't work.

Sara worries about her ability to arouse a man. And so she should if she expects to do this without using her greatest power: touch. Of the five senses, touch is the most powerful. Feeling his lover's touch will arouse her lover far more than what he sees, hears, smells, or tastes. The right touch, the one uniquely desired by him *will* excite him. If she is the lover giving him that touch, she will arouse him. All she has to do is learn what that touch is and give it to him. But of course that's a lot to learn.

The surprise of Day 2—Sara finds this exceedingly difficult. She lists more "problems" that keep her from touching her lover.

Sara:

> I never touch Barry, not in that way. Not anymore. Well, I'm not one of those aggressive women. I'm more feminine.

She used to "be all over him," *but* as they made love again and again and again, she did less:

- I don't do hand jobs anymore, I've . . . we've outgrown that.
- I don't think he wants me to touch him, he wants to get right down to fucking.
- Why should I touch him? I want to feel as though he is *crazy* to touch me . . . to feel as though he cares about me passionately . . . that he loves me more than anything . . . if I felt that, then I'd be all over him. I can't if I feel . . . yeah, he cares, but not that much.

She wants him to be *"crazy* to touch" her, *first.* He wants her to be wild to touch him, *first.*

Impasse.

Unfortunately Sara is preoccupied with the wrong problems.

- No need to know "what men want." Men all want different things.
- Rather than being aggressive, the erotic touch from a woman to a man is vitally feminine.
- The goal of the Ten-Day Plan is to take Sara beyond push-a-button, have-an-orgasm, paint-by-the-numbers mechanical sex by giving her a structure to find the erotic joys especially suited for Barry and Sara—lover to lover.

Their desire will follow the right touch. All they've ever had to do to be wildly erotic again is to learn to touch each other in the many ways that give them erotic pleasure.

Sara's goal: Touch Barry so Barry feels good. Every second she spends worrying about why touching him is so impossible, is time she spends avoiding doing the most important erotic act: touching Barry. Without her lover's touch, Barry is erotically deprived.

Sara:

> I do. I touch him. It's not like I never touch him. I give him hugs. I put my arms around Barry when we're making love.
>
> Anyway, I've been all over his body. I gave him a total massage once, but nothing much happened.

It wouldn't. The heavy massage touch relaxes muscles. Erotic touch excites. And can only be discovered one way: from the lover.

Sara tries to find out. The skin she touches tells her nothing. The information she gets from his general body tension is minimal. He appears relaxed. She looks into his eyes. He appears ... she can't tell. He isn't saying anything, so he must like it. But now Sara has doubts. Both lovers stare intently at the skin on the back of his hand. It's as though they are waiting for the skin to speak. It does not. (Neither does the skin on his penis or the skin on his testicles.)

They are animals of a higher order, and yet, when they make love, Sara and Barry behave as though they were just animals; they give up their power of speech. And when they do speak the words are so general they are of little use.

Nothing new in this experience. She fails to find out much for the same reasons neither of them ever find out much when they make love. Every time she asks, "Is this okay?" he gives the standard "after-lovemaking" answer; he gives *her* standard answer: "I like everything. Anything you do is fine." An answer which Barry feels sure is encouraging, but which puts Sara at a tremendous disadvantage. She still has no idea how to touch her lover to give him *more* pleasure.

Lovers' Questions

To get a better answer she needs a better question. If it's the *specific* touch that is the most erotic, Sara needs a question that Barry must answer specifically.

The Best Question: *Which is better?*

Better. Never best. No need to find out the best touch, the best touch is final and leads to repetition and to satiation and right back to low desire. The better touch at the present sensual moment leaves the lovemaking open. Sara asks:

> Which do you like better?
> Do you like this?
> Or this?
> Or that?

Which allows Barry to do something new: he discriminates *among* erotic pleasures.

> Fingertips are better.
> Softer is better.
> Up and down is better.
> I like to feel your fingers softly on my palms. My palms are very
>   sensitive.

Hands-on-Hands Learning

Sara puts her hand on top of his. With her fingers between her lover's fingers, Sara can feel exactly how he touches himself. She knows the movement, the pressure, the speed, at the instant he knows it.

Barry:
> I can make intricate movements, move in ways that I would find difficult to describe. Well, I couldn't describe the exact movements too well in words.

With the Best Question and Hands-on-Hands Learning as tools, Sara discovers fourteen new erotic pleasures that she can give her lover, and on the third day he discovers eighteen he can give her. All of which generate erotic thoughts these lovers had long ago abandoned.
Sara discovers that Barry wants her to

—Touch his new body in new ways:

> I have such surprising things to put on my list. He wants me to hold his hand. He never told me that, because he thought if I wanted to, I just would and since I didn't, that meant I didn't want to, but I could have been holding his hand for the last couple of years, all he had to do was tell me what he wanted. I learned seven different ways to touch his palms. He likes me to lean real close to him when I'm touching him. Part of what makes him feel good is to feel my body warm and close to his.

—In new surroundings:

> I hadn't thought about Sara's clothes for a long, long time. I . . . well . . . I knew it was my turn to get what I wanted and I thought of Sara wearing long, pale blue, silk pajamas . . . just the bottoms, no tops. I was really looking forward to that so I bought her some. . . . Good god, does she look great topless. . . . I like to fuck early . . . early in the morning . . . after work and late at night, I'm still . . . in my head . . . half at work. I asked her to look in my eyes.

That makes it nice for me. I've felt sometimes that she was somewhere else.

—Which generates new thoughts:

> I like this closeness and, what can I tell you, it's a relief to fool around and feel good and not have to put on a whole performance every time. I keep thinking about Sara wearing those long, pale blue, silk pajamas . . . I keep thinking of her bare breasts . . . the little dimple next to her right nipple.

Day 3: He Touches Her Legs

Barry discovers Sara wants him to

—Touch her new body in new ways:

> She likes me to slide my hand along the soles of her feet, to slide my oily fingers between her toes, to pay the most attention to her soft inner thighs, where she gets highly aroused. She can distinguish eight different erotic touches on her inner thighs. She likes me to slap her thigh, leave my hand in place, and then tease with my fingertips. She gets a sexual flush when I oil the creases at the back of her knees.

—In new surroundings:

> She likes cucumber soap.

—Which generates new thoughts:

> I was thinking about his hands on the inside of my thighs, his warm oily hands, those hands with the tender palms.

Day 4: She Touches His Legs

She smooths lotion high on the inside of his thigh, repeats the motion, and both lovers do what is excruciatingly common—but completely irrational. They look at his penis to see how his thigh feels.

Looking for the erection signal. Warning. The erection that announces desire may lie. Barry could be experiencing a fantastic sensual feeling in his thigh and have no erection. Or he could have a giant erection and hate the way his lover touches his thigh. During those moments searching for the erection, Sara and Barry work so hard they block the sensual feeling of the instant. Her fingers against his thigh might be a wonderful sensual moment. But Sara and Barry are not there to enjoy it.

Words bring them back.

Sara:
     You don't like this too much, do you?

Barry:
     I do like it. Don't stop. A bit heavier. Feels super. I want to feel that more.

Without words, Sara would have looked at his penis and decided Barry didn't want her to touch his thigh and she wouldn't have touched him like that ever again.

On Day 4 Sara discovers Barry wants her to

—Touch his new body in new ways:

     He likes me to caress the tops of his feet. He wants me to walk my fingers across the sensitive creases at the back of his knees. He loves me to lick his thigh. He wants me to suck his toes.

—In new surroundings:

     He likes to roll around on satin and fur. He wants perfume on my nipples, a long gold chain hanging between my breasts.

—Which generates new thoughts:

     I was thinking about being with Sara all day at the bakery ... about feeling her hands on my body ... about spending some time ... maybe doing something corny like playing "Bolero" and licking each other till we die.

Desire

Day 5: He Touches Her Body (Excluding Genitals)

She wants him to

—Touch her new body in new ways:

> I did everything she wanted and she got so sexed up, what can I tell you, she's crazy for me. I kissed her eyes. I licked her eyelids. I pulled her hair upward and bit the back of her neck. I oiled her spine with the ends of my fingers. I circled her bellybutton with my tongue, wider and wider circles, darting in and out. She was moaning and carrying on. . . . The word. . . . Her main word was "more."

—In new surroundings:

> I wrapped her body in a big warm towel, Sara inside a warm towel inside plastic, me unwrapping parts of her and touching and licking and biting.

—Which generates new thoughts:

> When Barry touches me like that I feel so loved.

Day 6: She Touches His Body (Excluding Genitals)

Sara discovers that Barry wants her to

—Touch his new body in new ways:

> I ran my nails through the hair on his chest, I did a lot with my tongue. Barry is real fond of my tongue . . . my tongue on his stomach . . . I licked him behind the ears, I would run my fingers over his lips, lick his lips, then put my fingers in his mouth, then put my tongue in his mouth. I would lie over him and touch his chest with my nipples.

—In new surroundings:

> I put every mirror in the house on chairs, lined up around the bed. We could see all parts of our bodies.

—Which generates new thoughts:

> I was thinking about Sara's eyes. They turn a brighter green
> when she gets to really liking what we do in bed. I admit I made a
> mistake about her . . . she does want to experiment. I spend half the
> day thinking about her . . . about how I want to get to her . . . to
> play around with her like we did in the beginning.

Of course, what must happen, happens. The lovers experience new
bodies, new touch, new surroundings, and new erotic thoughts which
increase their desire and increase it again.

Barry and Sara are a rousing sexual success even before they touch each
other's genitals.

Day 7: He Touches Her Genitals

Directions for Him on How to Explore His Lover's Vagina: Start at the
mouth of the vagina and imagine an outer third, a middle third, and an
inner third. Imagine the circle of the inside of the vagina divided like a
clock so that 12 o'clock starts below the bellybutton.

Barry:

> I found some lumpy lines from the middle third to the outer
> third at six o'clock. May have been scars from the baby. I touched
> them lightly. No response. I touched them harder and harder. She
> couldn't feel anything. It was like the area was anesthetized. She
> felt a little, but not much in the middle and the deepest part of her
> vagina. It was the deepest part that I was going to go for . . . I al-
> ways imagined if I got in *real* deep she would go wild . . . and some-
> times she does, but it isn't because she's feeling much there. Really.
> It's the outer third of her vagina near the entrance where she is
> really sensitive . . . near the vaginal opening from the left to the
> right in a half circle under her bellybutton.
>
> When I pressed there real hard she felt an erotic sensation in her
> clitoris. The area was sensitive and I could see that forcing the en-
> trance of her vagina open like that pulled the skin around her clit
> so she was going for two feelings—one in her clit and another in
> her vagina.

46

Her breasts are real sensitive ... and her clit ... well ... too rough at first turns her off *completely,* but she likes circles around the outside. When you come to think of it, it's just like my old man said, girls *are* different than boys.

On the seventh day Barry discovers that Sara wants him to

—Touch her new body in new ways:

> She put my hand on her breast. I love the feel of her wanting me to touch her ... it's totally beyond being excited. Her nipples are already all stuck out and she wants me to run my fingers over her nipples like I was going over a picket fence, tip, tip, tip. When I kiss her nipples, she wants me to use my tongue, and do different sucking motions. I run my tongue along the crease where her ass and her legs come together. She likes little light ass kisses, real near and all around her anus.
>
> Sara wants a light touch around the lips of her cunt and heavy pressure ... she wants me to push my fingers hard ... hard and fast ... inside her vagina.
>
> It's the clit, fingers on the clit really get to her. She likes quick, light, soft around her clit, back and forth using different rhythms.

—In new surrroundings:

> I put perfume on her breasts. Lipstick on the nipples.

—Which generates new thoughts:

> I was thinking about having sex with Barry standing up in the closet. Door closed. Me back in the corner. He's undressing after work, hanging up his coat and shirt and belt and slacks ... and I'm just there and he keeps undressing and fucks me.

Day 8: She Touches His Genitals

Barry:

> I don't think she's going to want to touch my cock. There was a time after we started living together ... she stopped touching me

... stopped touching my cock. I suspected she had changed but then one night ... it was one of those great moments in sports ... I put her hand on my penis ... and she said, "I don't do hand jobs anymore. . . ." I kept kissing her ... and after that ... I let go of her ... kept my distance more and more. She's got such a negative attitude.

Cautious talk from a man whose lover has a history of not wanting to touch his penis. No need.

By the eighth day, Sara is a new lover full of questions.

Which touch do you like better on your penis? Softer? Stronger? Would you like lotion? How much? How much pressure do you like on your penis? Do you prefer just the base be held? What touch do you like at the tip? Would you like your whole penis to be held? How would you like your penis stroked? Would you like me to move my hands up and down your penis? At what rate? Would you like a continuous stroke? Would you like me to stop and start? How long between touches? Do you like me to lick your penis? Do you like me to put your penis in my mouth? Just the tip? The length? Do you like my tongue on the underside of your penis?

On the eighth day Sara discovers that Barry wants her to

—Touch his new body in new ways:

Barry wants me to fool around with his nipples ... and with the purple part around the anus opening. He likes a real light touch on his ass ... and slaps ... spanks. He wants heavy touch, moving my hand back and forth between his scrotum and his anus. His testicles are totally sensitive. I hold his balls apart ... gentle and increase the pressure ... real slow ... like when I'm kissing him or fooling around with his anus.

I'd been using my tongue all over his body so it seemed real natural to touch his penis that way ... to use my tongue and my mouth. Barry used to thrust in my mouth so hard it scared me and I wouldn't do it anymore ... but he likes to feel my hand real tight around the base of his penis. It gets him higher and I feel totally comfortable and can get down to enjoying the taste of his wonderful soft, stiff dick.

—In new surroundings:

> He brought home white satin sheets . . . and a red light bulb for the bedroom. We lay in the living room in front of the fire on these satin sheets . . . and I fed him grapes . . . and he got a new kind of condom with ridges . . . and after I discovered twenty or thirty things he liked, we got drunk and filled the rubbers with water and played ball . . . naked.

—Which generates new thoughts:

> Touching without penetration . . . this erotic stuff is getting to me. I need all my will power to keep from ejaculating. A week ago I was so bored I sometimes wondered if I was going to get it up . . . and now . . . I am not even in her yet . . . and I have to ask her to stop.
>
> I was thinking about anal intercourse. Driving to work I saw myself oiling her anus, playing with my fingers in and out, relaxing her, getting her real high, till she was totally begging me to give it to her in the ass.

Day 9: He Discovers Which Touch, Positions, and Movements She Likes Better During All Genital Activity, Including Penis-in-the-Vagina Intercourse

Day 10: She Discovers Which Touch, Positions, and Movements He Likes Better During All Genital Activity, Including Penis-in-the-Vagina Intercourse

As they add penetration and thrusting, they hold to the original goal: to find out which touch feels better.

The Right Touch for Higher Desire

The first discovery: *As their desire builds, they want the touch to change.* He likes one kind of touch at the beginning, different touch as he builds, and yet a third variety of touch as he nears orgasm. So does Sara.

49

Lover to Lover

He discovers that she wants him—

at the beginning:
—to give again all those touches he has just learned to give to her body and to add more
—to kiss her spine
—to caress her pubic hair
—to run his fingers in circles around her nipples
—to continue caressing her breasts until she lubricates

after arousal is established:
—to increase her arousal by penetrating while she is on her stomach
—to lick her nipples; to suck her nipples; to try tongue variations on her breast; to bite her breasts
—to play with her clitoris; to trace his fingers around the edges of her clitoris; to lick her clitoris
—to thrust for a while and then stop
—to change positions and thrust again

as she nears orgasm:
—to hold her so tight that she can barely breathe
—to increase the pressure and the speed of his fingers on her clitoris; to withdraw his hand just before she orgasms
—to thrust more vigorously
—to continue touching or sucking her breasts

She discovers that he wants her—

at the beginning:
—to give the body touches she has just learned
—to hold his testicles apart
—to put his limp penis in her mouth, to hold it, to suck gently

after becoming aroused:
—to lick his lips
—to tongue his stomach
—to hold his penis tighter as he becomes erect
—to pull his testicles back a little, and then down
—to match his increased arousal with more pressure to his testicles

as he nears orgasm:
—to stimulate the tip of his penis
—to raise her pelvis to match his rhythm

During penis-in-the-vagina intercourse the lovers become more nearly one and their discoveries blend:

> When I pressed my pelvis against him he could feel my vaginal muscles close around his penis. I released, then held tight. Touching him several places at the same time really increased his arousal. We found we like a side-to-side position; I get the best feeling with my leg across his back. My vagina is real sensitive in the front closest to the belly so we tried me on top, which was real good ... got so great when he was thrusting and also sucking my breast the way I had told him I liked ... and then he fingered my clit just like I like and ... and then we were going for it ... the perfect high.

> I knew which part of her vagina was most sensitive. I just penetrated deep and thrust back and forth, fingering her clit. I love hav-

50

ing her breasts hanging there right above my mouth. Side-to-side I penetrate shallow . . . sometimes she's got her hand around the base of my penis while I'm going in and out . . . sometimes I put her hand on her clit. . . . She's a wild lady . . . she gets even wilder when I penetrate while she is on her stomach.

These lovers are not used to telling each other what they feel, but when they do, every secret they reveal brings them closer.

Barry:

We are two new people. When you come to think of it, after all these years it is strange to daydream about how I want to get to . . . well this startling new Sara.

Sara:

His hands know my body . . . and they keep knowing it more. I can't wait to feel his hands all over me.

After ten days, what Barry and Sara have found is not the "best" way to make love. Instead they have found many ways. They have found the many ways of making love that makes each time new—as it was in the beginning.

Lovemaking as It Was in the Beginning

They have the techniques which allow them to go on discovering each other forever. As the months pass Sara and Barry report new and wonderful erotic discoveries.

His Sensitive Spot

Sara:

I found a real sensitive spot underneath the tip of his penis. I practiced getting my fingers just right, then I practiced again with my tongue. I put his whole penis in my mouth and sucked gently using my tongue on the underside all around his sensitive spot. I said, "Does this feel better . . . or lighter like this?"

He likes me to hold his testicles still with one hand . . . so they feel real secure . . . and he likes me to touch them real lightly with my other hand while I keep his penis in my mouth and tongue all around the sensitive spot.

Getting Too High

Barry:

I started with her toes . . . oiling upward . . . up and down the thighs . . . hand on the beautiful ass . . . fingers between the buttocks . . . circling the anus . . . Sara shivers . . . when you come to think of it, there's a reason I always want to get my hands on her ass . . . she's got one hell of a sensitive ass. . . . I dragged my fingers up her spine . . . rolled my body over hers . . . I was getting slick from her body . . . my penis between her ass . . . my hands stroking up and down . . . over her body . . . around her breasts . . . over her nipples . . . more oil on her clit . . . oil mixing with the wet of her vagina . . . fingers on the lips of her vagina . . . circling the clit . . . tongue in her mouth . . . her hands on my cock . . . my hands on her clit . . . I remember oil and sweat and getting too high . . . lying beside each other naked . . . my taking each of her fingers and putting mine around them sliding up and down . . . licking her slick nipple relaxing . . . she fell asleep with her lips on my pubic hair. . . .

Whipped Cream

Barry:

I got this idea . . . it was at the bakery . . . watching some guy with the whipped cream. So, what can I tell you, I took home ten cans. I licked Sara in places she'd never been licked.

Sex in the Water

Sara:

I circled the tub with candles, lit the incense, filled the bathtub with warm water and bubbles.

I undressed Barry . . . ran my hands over the hair on his chest . . . I love the feel of the hair on his chest . . . kissed his hair . . . on his chest . . . behind his ears . . . around his penis . . . on his testicles. . . . He kept his hands in my panties . . . his fingers twisting around through my pubic hair. I just want to help you, ma'am, he would say.

It's getting bothersome . . . getting so high . . . I didn't want to come in the first five minutes. I locked his hands around my waist . . . sat between his legs . . . turned facing him . . . slid under the water and nibbled his testicles . . . kissed him all the way . . . up his chest . . . his neck . . . over his chin . . . the end of his nose. Then I lay back between his legs. So warm. He wiped the bubbles off my face . . . put a warm towel around my shoulders. We lay quiet. My hands on his thighs. His hands around my waist . . . feeling the water . . . real relaxed. I felt his erection. I felt his skin . . . the connection between us. Seemed like our two bodies would always be connected in lovers' ways.

Coming on Her Breasts

Barry:

Sara was on the patio rolling around in the hammock with me . . . drinking lemonade . . . unzipped my shorts . . . playing with my cock . . . lazy Sunday. I kissed her underarm . . . licked the edges . . . the sensation in my cock . . . grew strong . . . I could see her naked breasts through her pink gauze shirt . . . I wanted her breasts and my cock . . . some way . . . and one thing led to another . . . and I was rubbing my cock over her nipples . . . rubbing my cock between her breasts . . . her breasts slick, oiled, warm against the sides of my cock . . . up and down . . . warm oiled breasts until I came . . .

sperm mixed with the oil on her breasts . . . I rubbed my come over her slick breasts . . . I thought I'd die. . . .

The Testicle High

Sara:

He had told me that he likes his testicles held, but I always pretended I didn't hear . . . or made a joke because I was afraid to touch him there. Guys' testicles are supposed to be so delicate and I always thought if you do anything wrong they'd faint, so even with his guidance I was sure I was going to hurt him. What happened was . . . I did what he said. . . . I ran my fingers back and forth between his anus and his testicles; I held his testicles gently separate; pulled down and he had the most ecstatic look I've ever seen him have—ever.

Barry:

She pulls down on my testicles which tightens the skin of my penis which gets me extremely excited. When you come to think of it, I almost lose my connection with reality. My reality is the erotic sensation. With the skin around my penis so tight what I feel on my cock, her tongue or her hand or her fingers, is heightened. I become supersensitive to the subtlety of the touch.

She never hurt me. At some time the pressure on my testicles would get near the borderline of pain. I thought it might really hurt, but it never did. I felt as though I was on a pleasure ride. As long as the force of the touch was just below the pain threshold I was wild. I love it.

With each intimate touch the lovers grow closer. He wants more. She wants more. They look for opportunities to sit close. They hold hands. Sometimes she wakes up in the middle of the night and finds him sound asleep kissing her. In their waking hours, they smile at each other. They look into each other's eyes. They are highly aroused. Lustful for each other.

They have found a secret world—lover to lover.

The Man Who Lost All
Desire for His Wife

"I have not made love to Cynthia for two years. I don't know what hap-
pened. Whatever was there is dead. Worse. I look at Cynthia and it's as
though I'm looking at a one-hundred-year-old woman."

Jack used to lust for Cynthia.

In the days when they were in Peace Corps training, all Jack thought
about was marrying Cynthia. He did. They worked in a small African
village, where their now seven-year-old daughter was born with Cynthia
attended by a midwife and Jack. Jack and Cynthia had been through a lot
together. Now they are back in the states—teaching. There are money
problems. He is up for tenure at his college, but has been too busy with
community work and work with students to abide by the unwritten rules
of his department—publish a book. Cynthia teaches multiculture studies
at a local junior college. Her job is funded by the government, and the
funds will be cut at the end of the year.

Everyone Jack and Cynthia know knows about their work in Africa,
about their extreme fondness for each other, about their money problems—but no one knows that Jack refuses to sleep with Cynthia. Or that
Cynthia has been unfaithful.

Cynthia thought when she slept with another man while her husband spent an additional year alone in Africa doing research that Jack would understand. She thought he might have even had an affair himself. She thought their marriage could withstand an "incident caused by the special circumstances of a long separation." Jack is furious, humiliated. He takes himself out of the male competition for his sexy wife.

How?

He relabels her.

> You remind me of a one-hundred-year-old woman.
> You are undesirable.
> I do not want you, Cynthia.

The incident that triggered Jack's loss of desire is past history. Since that time Cynthia has not been near another man, but she was unfaithful. That can never change. Two years later Jack and Cynthia are left with a major problem: Jack has lost all desire for his wife.

His desire loss is far more serious than the simple desire loss experienced by long-time lovers. Jack's desire loss is a distinctive type—the type that is often referred to by sex therapists when they say desire loss is the most difficult of all sexual problems to cure.

The distinction: Jack's desire loss has become part of his very language. Loving words have been replaced by hostile words. Words that reject Cynthia. Too many words are hostile and his lover retaliates. As the months go by the lovers are locked in a deadly dance. He drives her away; she drives him away. And they don't know how to stop.

Jack:

> Desire is such a mystery. I don't know how it happened. I just lost interest. Quite frankly, I feel terrible about this. I admit it. I love Cynthia, I love our family. I want to keep the family together. I would do anything and, quite frankly, I know this is awfully hard on Cynthia. We can't go on forever this way. I wish to God I could feel something for her. Quite frankly, I know if we can't change things I'm going to lose her.

The payoff: Since desire loss is beyond my control I don't have to do anything to actually save my marriage. But, of course, Jack didn't just lose his desire, he threw it away.

Desire

Under his mask of innocence, Jack hides a secret: Cynthia is not the first woman he has loved for whom he has killed his desire. There has been a long list of women—his mother, his sister, his third-grade teacher, his high-school buddy's married sister. All women he loved but refused to desire. Just as he should.

Now Jack shifts his appropriate desire-killing skills to an inappropriate target—his wife. Jack rationalizes:

> I don't know. My wife just doesn't excite me. Quite frankly—and this is true—a man can't be excited by just anybody, he just can't.

Jack is right. The fact that a man "can't be excited by just anybody" distinguishes him from the lower animals.

Theoretically we could—if we were only biological creatures—be wanting to have sex with everyone all the time. Jack's body gives him that potential. Jack could be wanting to have sex with everyone he meets. He could have sex with his grandmother, his daughter, the man who comes to wash the windows, his boss, the babysitter, his best friend's wife, and his best friend. Nothing wrong with those choices. Biologically.

And, if humans were solely creatures of biology, we would have sex with any human who happened to be nearby at the moment we had the urge to have sex. But we do not have sex with the closest animal. We discriminate.

Because we function in a highly complex social structure, we go beyond the mere biological. We select socially appropriate lovers. We channel our sexual desire toward those lovers we label socially appropriate.

We *learn* whom to desire. We learn to feel desire for those creatures of our own species who are unrelated by birth, of the opposite sex, and the same general age. Add some similarities of interests or personality or a particular shade of watery-blue eyes, and one finds one's great true love. Powerful social forces demand that we take our desire beyond our biology so we learn to inhibit. From a young age, Jack is told:

· No, you can't marry Mommy, Mommy is already married.
· No, honey, Aunt Mary and Barbara aren't going to get married.

57

Girls don't marry girls. Girls marry boys. Mary and Barbara are just best friends.

· Old enough to be his mother, she's old enough to be his grandmother, there can't be anything going on between that woman and your brother. After all, she's his *teacher*.

And so Jack listens, and learns to inhibit his sexual desire for people he loves.

There is for each of us a large group of humans with whom we allow ourselves to feel desire; another group with whom we inhibit desire. We don't *think* about it. Like Jack, most of us have no idea we're even *doing* anything. We believe that desire just happens *to* us. Of course, I don't want to have sex with my sister, or my brother's ten-year-old son. *That's unnatural!* Of course, I don't want to have sex with her—she's my principal, too old for me, a married woman. *I have no desire.* And, of course, I'm interested in Cynthia—she lives next door, goes to my high school, my age, parents like mine, she's . . . well, she's sexy. A man's attraction to a woman *requires* him to allow his sexual thoughts about her to develop.

Desire is something we make happen. If desire were a natural occurrence beyond our control—like our biology—desire would never be a problem. Whatever animal we naturally desired to have sex with would be the right animal. But desire is learned. And, because we learn it, some of us get it wrong. We are supposed to divide our desire: we inhibit our desire to one group; we expand our desire to another group. The problem for us comes when we get the wrong people in the wrong group.

Having learned to inhibit all too well, by the time we hit fifteen, most of us are experts, carrying with us the equivalent of a doctorate in the art of killing our desire. Most of us—like Jack—never desire people we shouldn't; that's not the problem. The problem is that we learn too well how to kill our desire.

And any one of us—like Jack—can learn to kill our desire for a woman who deserves our love.

How?

With our minds.

Although Jack is right, "a man can't be excited by just anybody," he leaves out one important fact: Cynthia isn't just anybody. She is a woman for whom he has pledged his love for eternity. Now, Jack kills his desire for Cynthia in the classic way we all kill our desire for sexually inappropriate people: he stops thinking of Cynthia as sexy.

We understand that beauty is in the eye of the beholder, but we often fail to realize how desire is in the mind of the lover. Jack closes his mind.

How Jack loses desire for the women he loves:

1. He does not let himself think about what makes her sexy.
2. When she kisses him he ignores his erotic response to her. He doesn't let that response grow.
3. When she offers to do things for him he labels her interest in him as platonic—sisterly.
4. If he sees her in her bra and panties, he doesn't let himself imagine her in sexual terms.
5. If she buys new lingerie, he teases her about wanting to look sexy—for *someone else.* His language begins to drive her away.
6. When they are alone together—he stops himself from having any thoughts of what they might do sexually.
7. When they are with other people, he invites the friends to stay, since he and Cynthia have no interest in having time or privacy for sex.
8. When he hugs her he carefully avoids feeling her breasts ... the message is, she's not sexual.
9. He never speaks to her about sexual things.
10. He ruminates to himself: "I wonder why nothing Cynthia does excites me," and with enough rumination, it doesn't.

By closing his mind toward her he controls his sexual desire—and Cynthia's.

Meeting for a romantic dinner in earlier days before Jack began to ruminate about his wife's affair, Cynthia spreads her arms wide, runs to grab him, and hugs her lover with all her might. Jack smiles, hugs back, kisses, pushes his tongue between her lips; Cynthia protests, "Not in public!" A fiercely sexual eye contact takes them through dinner, and the lovers rush home to make love.

Then, one day, Cynthia spreads her arms wide, grabs her husband; Jack coughs, and coughs, excuses himself, says that is so sweet of her, coughs again. During dinner, he talks about losing his job; after dinner she goes to bed early with a book. Two weeks later she spreads her arms wide and runs toward her husband. Jack stops her:

> You know, I never told you, but I've never felt right about hugging in public. Quite frankly, it's a little embarrassing to me. I mean, I feel a little embarrassed. I hope this doesn't hurt your feelings—I mean, quite frankly, we don't have to make a public display. We know we love each other.

Meeting for dinner, after six weeks of Jack's rejection of her advances, Cynthia keeps her arms at her side. Unable to show him affection, she loses some desire.

In the beginning of the romance Cynthia and Jack spent much of their erotic life talking about her underwear. He let her know how he liked to see her in and out of it. She would slide over his body—until he couldn't stand it—slide away from him; he would chase—and catch—her in the bathroom, the living room, the kitchen—in playful love.

Cynthia buys a soft, silky, silver camisole that sets off her red hair, sits on her lover's lap with a flirtatious smile. He says: "Are you trying to look sexy or something?" A small voice replies, "Yes." Feeling rejected, she loses more desire.

When Cynthia approaches him weeks later, Jack is ready with a new idea for her: stay away.

> You know I don't need any more pressure. I don't want to feel I have to *do* anything sexual. Quite frankly, I think it's best for us to distance for a few weeks—we'll be back to our old selves. You'll see.

They do, but Jack is wrong. Distance creates further distance. And after this separation has been engineered, Jack loses more desire. So does Cynthia. His payoff: separation prevents any small movement toward intimacy.

His language changes. Initially, he speaks in anger and he withdraws. Then the hostile words become an entrenched part of his relationship with her. The new hostile language, fed by her hostile reactions, becomes the way they stay apart. Jack doesn't see it that way.

> Of course, she's mad. I told her some women look kind of cute when they're mad, but she just looks ugly. Well, I believe you have to be honest. I told her, well, quite frankly, she hasn't excited me for quite a while. It's not her fault. It's just the way it is.

With that "honest" speech, Jack drives his wife farther away.

However, with all his cleverness at shoving his lover away, Jack has forgotten something: not only is sex in the mind, it's in the body. Mind and body connect. For two years Jack systematically relabels every sexual interaction with Cynthia as nonsexual. For two years he withdraws from sensual contact with her. He denies all sexual feeling; obliterates every sexual thought of her from his mind. Relabels every interchange as non-sexual. So, quite naturally, his body responds. Jack loses his ability to get an erection.

Jack tolerates two years of marital woe rather well, but impotence frightens him. The doctor he consults finds that during sleep his erections are perfect; his impotence is caused by anxiety. The first steps of treatment:

- Temporarily stop any attempt at penis-in-the-vagina intercourse so you can concentrate on reestablishing positive erotic thoughts, positive erotic words, positive erotic touch.
- Stay erotically close to your lover. Allow your lover to caress your body in slow stages—arms and hands for half an hour. Allow warm feelings to build. Allow sexual thoughts to expand. Allow yourself to use language to label what touch you find more pleasurable. Allow yourself to feel desire.
- Give the lover options, pay attention to details, give him the touch he wants.

Impotence caused by lack of desire—in cases of long standing in which the husband has relabeled the wife as inappropriate—is difficult to treat because the treatment forces the two lovers into erotic contact. Normally, two lovers working together are unbeatable. That's why there are such high cure rates for all sex problems—*except total loss of desire for a once-loved lover.*

Two reasons why Jack's desire loss is so difficult to cure. 1) To keep hold of total desire loss, Jack must reject Cynthia—in thought, word, and touch. It's a rare lover who can withstand sexual rejection *without retaliating*. 2) Having labeled Cynthia sexually off-limits, if he is to keep her there Jack must destroy the treatment. The treatment is structured to slowly bring Cynthia closer to him. He feels he must stop this from happening.

It's like this. You are a man whose eighteen-year-old daughter is gorgeous. Young men chase after her; older men stare at her. You see her beauty, her sexiness, and you are proud. But. For years you have built a system of sexual prohibitions against feeling, thinking, touching. Sexually, she is off-limits. The idea is unthinkable. What if your doctor told you—for some unfathomable reason—to let your daughter soap you in a warm bath, let her touch your arm and hand like a lover, to let her relax you into an intimate, warm sensuality. What if you were ordered to think about having sex with her? You would feel repelled. You would hate it. You would want to avoid such a situation. You would want her to stop touching you like that. The strain to feel nothing sexual would exhaust you. You would want to get away because your thoughts about your daughter are all nonsexual and you want to keep them that way. You do not want to change.

You would, in fact, feel just like Jack. Except that your feelings would be appropriate to your social relationship with your daughter. Jack takes these same feelings and pastes them on an inappropriate woman—his wife.

> Quite frankly, doctor, I look at Cynthia and she looks to me . . . I feel like she is a one-hundred-year-old woman. Now, you tell me it's going to be good for me to have sex with this one-hundred-year-old woman. Okay, you said to do it, I'll try, but I don't think I'll be able to . . . quite frankly, I'm sure as hell not going to feel anything.

Jack has said he loves his wife and he would do anything to save his family—but asked to make one small change, he gets ready to sabotage the effort. Which is sad, because if he cannot change he will lose Cynthia. And the love they shared. And his family.

Five Tricks to Kill Your Desire

1. *Avoid touch.*
Touch increases your arousal. Touch provides pleasure and leads to positive sensual words, leads you to think of her as sexual. Don't let this happen. If you absolutely must touch, be sure it is at the worst possible time.

Jack:

> At the beginning of the week, Cynthia was enthusiastic. She suggested several times that she was ready, but I was tired. I sleep every night after work, until about ten, sometimes midnight. Then one night she was tired, and I said we'd better do something. So I told Cynthia that she could wake me up any time that night. It was about one thirty in the morning when I woke up. Cynthia had gone to bed . . . was sound asleep. . . .
> Quite frankly, by this time when I finally got her awake about two A.M. I don't think she could concentrate.

2. *Promptly label each lover's touch nonsexual.*
Sensing danger, Jack quickly relabels his experiences. The warm bath and the caring caress which would make most lovers feel warmth, tenderness, and gentle pleasure becomes "this mechanical thing." "This mechanical thing" is "not to be taken seriously."
Following this line, he relabels with jokes. Triple payoff on this one. 1) Jokes, in and of themselves, always lower arousal by obliterating the present sensual moment. 2) These particular jokes about erections and orgasms lower arousal by placing the lovers' past failures in the center of their present thoughts. 3) The jokes carry a hidden message to the lovers—*what you feel now doesn't count.*

> Well, I made some jokes . . . we all know this mechanical thing isn't anything to get too heavy about . . . so she was feeling my leg, and I said, "Cynthia, you're really a leg girl, huh?" And then I

would say, "Hey, kid, do you think I'm getting a leg-on?" . . . I did make her break up. I turned a blank face to her and said, absolutely deadpan: "Well, did you come?"

More nonsexual labels. Rather than speak of penis, dick, balls, or even of arms and legs, Jack removes himself farther and farther from his body. He calls his body parts "extremities" and "sexual organs." Jack finds it "unnatural to pay attention to an extremity that is not a sexual organ." Nothing sexual in that phrase. He has closed his mind. No penis on his body. Not even an arm or a leg. So much less likely to feel loved on one's "extremity."

3. *Never tell your lover what feels good or what doesn't, so she won't be able to speak with you about sensual things.*
If you truly feel uncomfortable because of something that could easily be remedied, decide it isn't worth telling your lover. Avoid the words that could bring you close.

> Well, the house was a little cool, and I was feeling clammy, a little uncomfortable. Well, I was shivering. I didn't tell Cynthia because, quite frankly, it wouldn't serve any purpose. At that time of night, there was nothing she could do. And I didn't want to put her in that position—asking her for something when there was nothing she could do.

At one point Jack nearly admits that he liked the feel of her body close to him, that he liked the general feel of care. Cynthia softens and is about to touch his knee. And Jack kills the moment:

> Quite frankly, she was unfaithful on a number of occasions, and I can't stop thinking about that. I know she is angry about my impotence—she has every right.

Cynthia leaps to the bait:

> No, I didn't ask him what touch he liked, what good are those details? Why pay attention if he can't have sex anyway?

64

And the lovers are off. Jack is so much less likely to feel desire once he makes sure there is nothing this woman can do that will make him feel closer to her.

4. *Convince your lover that touching you is useless.*

This is essential. Sensual nondemanding, nonperformance touch is the most effective way to build desire. To kill desire, you must tell your lover that you dislike her each and every touch. Tell her that every touch makes you feel terrible. Give details of just how terrible.

Jack's biggest problem is right here. Now he is pushed up against reality. It's terribly difficult to hold that stance: I feel nothing for my passionate, voluptuous lover as she spends half an hour caressing me tenderly in this warm, slippery, sensual way. Constantly afraid of losing the battle, Jack struggles against feeling closer to her, until he becomes so anxious he wants to leap out of his skin.

> Five minutes. That's it. If she touches me more than five minutes I want to get away. I feel itchy. I want to be somewhere else. I would feel better watching television. I could read a book. I could be out of the house . . . I don't like this. When I'm in the tub I think, This is annoying. The soap is going to get in my eyes. I hope this is over quickly. Her hand feels creepy on my skin. . . . I had to be honest—the most I could say was that some parts were a little less comfortable.
>
> Quite frankly, the situation is a bit embarrassing to me. I'm a person who is not used to that kind of attention.
>
> I mean, being touched *very slowly* with those questions: How does it feel? Is this fast enough? Slow enough? Is this wet enough? How do you like this? I am not used to that—that attention to detail. It does nothing for me. I don't like it.
>
> What I like . . . I like to be in bed with her when we can turn away from each other. In this mechanical thing, I had to keep looking at her, I had to answer questions.

Translation: The solution to my problem will *not* work. Don't try it. I'm telling you. There's no use doing anything.

5. *Reject your lover* before *you let her touch you.*

Reject her. Reject her. Reject her. His five tricks to kill desire boldly in effect, Jack waits for his lover's violent explosion. And he gets what he wants. Cynthia furiously accuses him of doing exactly what he has done.

> You avoid sex, you reject me, you wake me in the middle of the night, insult me, ask me to help you feel something and then you set the whole thing up so it's a farce. You only pretend you're try-ing, you just do it like it's a play, you make everything a joke, you keep telling me you hate my touch, you say sex is useless, I'm use-less. Well, I'm not a person who swears, but you can believe I mean this—"Fuck you. Fuck you, Jack."

The surprise: Jack agrees. Absolutely. In fact, his reaction to each part of his experience with his lover is perverse. As he speaks of feeling warm and caressed, he gets visibly tense, but when he supports his wife's com-plaints, he actually loosens up, his voice becomes warm and caring, al-most loving.

> She is resentful. She wants to get back at me. She feels hurt be-cause I don't want her. And now with "my inability" I feel kind of guilty. I don't blame Cynthia for feeling angry. She has every right.

This sympathy is diabolical. While supporting his wife's rightful com-plaints, he is reinforcing her anger, keeping her busy with angry thoughts, taking her farther away from any chance of reconciliation.

Jack is more powerful than the therapist. He has the will to fail. And he has made his rejected lover an accomplice. Working together to defeat the solution to their problem, they are invincible. Treatment to regen-erate Jack's desire focuses on the here and now. Jack and his lover are to start over—to have an affectionate, good feeling, through touch, as though they were two kittens snuggling about on a warm rug—no past, no future, no grudges, no expectations, no performance, just the feel of the moment. Jack and his lover refuse.

Impasse.

With even the slightest good feeling, the lovers could build. Lower an-imals are so close to their biology that they feel good at the first touch. But the higher animals have sophisticated brains that allow them to reject their natural feelings. They can lie, they can rationalize, they can paste past grievances over their present experience.

Human lovers can turn any touch into a repulsive, exhausting "mechanical thing." Erotic touch exists because of our ability to allow our erotic sensations to flourish. Given the best possible situation, each one of us has the higher-animal ability to suppress our sexual thoughts. Even put in the best situation and given the best instructions, we can refuse to feel. We can relabel. We can announce our lover's failure. We can pick a fight.

The consequences for human lovers, however, are far more serious than for the lower animals. Two years and six months after Jack lost his desire for his wife, she left him. She took their daughter to another state and, after a few years, she married a dentist who raised goats and rabbits. He was a big burly teddy bear of a man who smiled every time she touched him. They had two children. Jack saw his daughter two weeks each year for a while. When she was twelve she decided she no longer wanted to visit. Jack never remarried.

Although this willed loss of desire is a tough, tough problem, a strong person, a person with a will of iron, can survive—and, perhaps, save the relationship. Had Cynthia been strong enough to reject her lover's rejection, the marriage might have survived. He said he loved her. He said he would do anything to save the family. Given such a lover, a woman who truly believes can use five tricks of her own:

Five Tricks to Rescue the Lover Who Has Lost Desire

1. *Reject your lover's rejection.*

Rejection is the key. Jack's inappropriate rejection of Cynthia is the mainstay of his illness. She hears only his rejection. Reverse the order: hear only his statement of love. The rejection is part of the disease. If she can accept his rejection as a symptom of illness and try to combat its existence, she has the best chance to break the system.

Think of desire loss as a disease—similar to a biological disease. One can be outraged that germs have entered the body, one can take this as a personal insult, curse the god that would do such a vile thing, and declare that if this god causes germs to fill my body, then I'll just put more germs in my body. That's one option. Or, one can recognize the germ theory of disease, tell oneself that the germs, rather than being a personal insult, are to be expected, considering the disease—and work on bringing them under control.

Jack's rejection of Cynthia—like a germ—is to be expected, considering the disease. His rejection—being endemic to desire loss—needn't be taken personally, and will end once the disease is brought under control.

Only a very strong individual can withstand the onslaught. The lover who can ignore sexual rejection—even when love is professed—may have the possibility of success within her grasp, if she understands that ignoring his hostile words leads to success.

Hearing her lover's rejection, Cynthia should have slid by her own anger and said: "I care about you."

2. *Touch.*
At the best times. Often. Reverse action. Instead of allowing your lover to engineer sensual situations for the worst times, engineer him into the best situation.

Cynthia could have said:

> Darling, I know how tired you've been, so I've sent the little terror to mother's for the weekend. I've planned for us to have Sunday afternoon to be together.

Cynthia could have said:

> Darling, I love this party. But Gloria told me privately she wants to clear the place before midnight. She asked us to help her—so I said we'd go at ten thirty.

3. *Label your relationship sexual.*

Cynthia:

- I like the hair on your chest.
- Your thighs are so nice and hard.

- *I like the feel of your legs against my hand.*
- *Put your tongue against my lips. In my mouth. Come on, just a little.*

4. *Pay attention to the details of what he likes.*

No matter how small. No matter how badly he expresses them. Don't be distracted. Stay with the present moment.

He shivers.

Are you feeling too cool? Here, I'll warm the water.

If Jack had said:

Honestly, I don't *like* to be touched. Quite frankly, it all makes me feel intensely uncomfortable.

Then Cynthia might have said:

Does this feel *less* uncomfortable?

Or if Jack had said:

Oh come on, we shouldn't get so heavy about this mechanical thing. Quite frankly, you know it and I know it, I'm never going to get an erection from you fingering one of my extremities. I'm impotent, for God's sake, that's the problem.

Ideally she stays in the present:

Your hands feel so warm. I like them so silky and slippery. Do you think I could kiss the back of your knee? Do you like this? Or little bites, like this? Or little licks?

This is the trick that separates the women from the girls. If you are human, you will want to match his complaints, you will want to avoid your own anxiety through an escape hatch to past misery. If you do, you lose.

5. Believe that touching works.

Believe your touch *is* working, no matter what your lover says. He is wrong. His belief that touching him is useless is part of his illness. When he says, "All right, go ahead, but I don't *like* it," do what the man says, go ahead. Touch. Pay attention to details. Touch him the way he likes. The best strategy is to treat him as though he is what you say you want—your most desired lover. Touch him for long periods of time, paying close attention to detail, being close, shutting his grumbles out of your mind until he crumbles. Into your arms. And you go slowly, sensually, forward. To build trust. And desire.

IMPOTENCE
Doing the Right Things
to Get an Erection

I rolled close to her, unbuttoned her pajamas, and kissed her breasts; I put her hands around my penis. Her hands feel so good there, but I didn't get much of an erection, just a little one. I kissed her breasts, put my mouth around the nipples—licked and sucked. I could feel her getting excited. Then I shucked her out of her pajama bottoms, lay on top of her, rubbed my soft penis back and forth over her clitoral area. I could feel her body get hotter and hotter. I could hear her breath coming faster and faster. After two or three minutes she came.

After that, I asked her to play with me a little. She did. And we went to sleep.

John and Hilde have a life limited to one brief sex act: he rubs his soft penis against her clitoris till she has an orgasm. The act is neither outrageous nor perverse. As John and Hilde do it, it's an act of loving kindness. However, they can do nothing else.

Or rather, like many impotent couples, they don't *believe* they can do anything else. John's soft penis is just the way it is. It's mysterious. It's hopeless. Especially in John's case, they say, because he's been impotent for more than five years.

But actually time doesn't matter. In healthy men all erection failure is caused by the same thing—insufficient arousal. The next time John's arousal goes high enough he will get an erection.

That's old news, but nearly unknown news. The basic cure for impotence was published in the medical literature nearly two hundred years ago. That method has been refined by sex therapists over the past twenty years. Their success rates show that in a few weeks or months more than 80 percent of severely impotent men can learn to have erections again. The same techniques, moreover, work to help any man get an erection and keep an erection. Furthermore, the man who understands the techniques that cure impotence has something of great value. With this knowledge he can protect himself from becoming impotent in the first place.

Unfortunately, John and Hilde have been so distracted by the trauma of impotence they, like many couples, never think of doing things to effect a cure. They think of keeping the secret. When they speak of his soft penis, they whisper. They speak in a private language—"our way" is what they call what they do in bed. Impotence is a condition they find excruciatingly embarrassing. One they believe they have to hide.

To protect John's impotence, John's wife lies to him. "I don't miss intercourse because I like to feel his warm, soft penis between my legs. I get what I want 'our way.'" John lies to his wife: though he swears he has never had an erection with any woman in five years, he did get erections with his first wife. And he did try to get erections with a number of women, tried things that didn't work—things he could never tell Hilde—and each time he was left with a soft penis, an emotional wreck of a man, feeling humiliated.

It's their strong emotions that prevent lovers from overcoming erection failure. No reason to feel such strong emotions. Erections work a certain way in all men, and any man in the same circumstances who tried what John did would also have failed. Cause and effect was nothing personal, just male biology.

Caught up in these terrible emotions, in hushed tones Hilde tells the story of the first time they made love. Her face flushes. Her voice shakes. She whispers.

He told me he might have problems and when, after three weeks of dating, we went to bed he did have trouble. I found out ... there was trouble with John from that first day. He was so fearful that when he tried to make love to me his body turned sopping wet, the sheets, too, were wet through and through. I had never met a man with his problem. It was all new to me and I was very curious.

He got a little bit of an erection, but not enough for intercourse. Never for the past five years under any circumstances has he been able to get an erection. He tried. He and his first wife tried—but no erection. Besides his first wife, there was just me and a succession of women he would meet for just one night. Every time he failed, and then he was too afraid to try again.

It's far too emotional a subject to talk about. Naturally, none of their friends or relatives know. When John first started having trouble making love to Gail, his first wife, he took pains to see a doctor in another county. The doctor gave him a testosterone shot, told him to take a vacation, to relax. The shot had no effect, he wasn't the kind of man who found it easy to relax, and, as the erection failure continued, he never told Gail he had sought help. Now he and Hilde spend a lot of time pretending to each other that this problem that they take such pains to conceal really is no problem.

Like many impotent couples, they insist that "other things" are more important in a marriage. They say they have adjusted. And they keep their secrets.

Hilde's secret:

Sometimes I would like a little more. Sometimes I think of how it would be to feel a real man inside my body. I want a baby, but I'll never tell him.

John's secret:

After I felt comfortable with her, I put my hand on my penis to try to add something, but she took my hand away. She was so upset, said I shouldn't touch myself, that's what she should do—and she did, but she never gets it right. I let it go . . . I feel so . . . I want to be like other men. I want to have normal sex.

That's just the surface. There are other sexual secrets that John and Hilde hide so deep, they barely remember they are there.

John and Hilde tell their sex histories from the social point of view, leaving out the parts about how these events in their lives changed what they actually did sexually. After hearing each other's stories during courtship they both believe they know the previous sex activities of the other. They don't.

John:

My father's death turned me into an old man with grave responsibilities. At a young age I had to support my mother and my older sister at a higher standard than my father had provided for at his death. I could do nothing except work. I was afraid to speak to a girl. That might lead to my wanting to ask for a date. But I had no money to date, and no time, and I was terrified of an accidental pregnancy. I was afraid to have anything to do with women. I was holding up a financial load with very little base. Two more mouths to feed and the façade would be revealed for what it was.

My goal—take care of my mother, save money, make money, look neither to the left nor the right, never think about my needs. I worked . . . fourteen hours a day . . . eighteen hours a day . . .

After I had my own business—and it was going fairly well, I married the first woman I had sex with. My mother reacted badly. She went into a deep depression.

I had been divorced a long time when I met Hilde. I felt so lucky. She was the first woman in three years who said she didn't care whether or not I got erections, she cared about me. I married her very fast—before she changed her mind.

Hilde:

I always picked the wrong man. When I was young I married an alcoholic. Every day for three years of our marriage it was awful. No one would give me any help. His parents refused to believe that he drank.

After the divorce I lived with a man who was even worse. This second man didn't like to work. I paid for everything. He lived in my house, the house I bought with the help of my parents. He drove my car. It was very convenient for him. Then my parents stopped it. They sold the house from under me, sold all my stocks, sold my car, and I was left with nothing. As soon as my lover realized I was poor, he told me to go away. It was the worst time of my life. I did not know that this was what my parents wanted. My father saved every penny for me, and as soon as my lover was gone, my father gave me all the money.

From then on I was very careful. I'm different from his first wife. She couldn't take it. Sex, that's never been the most important aspect with me—I had plenty of regular sex with men who got erections and they left me miserable. My first husband . . . the man I lived with after my divorce . . . they hurt me so dreadfully I stayed away from men from the age of twenty-eight to thirty-two.

That was when I met John. He was handsome, a self-made man, charming. John talks to you as though you are of such special importance that extreme care must be taken with your fragile but precious ego. You leave a conversation with John feeling very good about yourself.

I married John because he is a good, kind man. Besides, I like "our way." I get what I want. He was the man I had waited for—a good man. A man of strong character. That is what is important to me. I am interested only in his character.

Hilde associates good sex with bad men, of whom she's had enough. She is almost eager to accept John's impotence. Besides, she has another secret.

John is afraid of my vagina. He's unable to touch me there. He's afraid of a woman's body. Something happened with his mother—years ago—when he was a little boy . . . that has left him . . . sexually . . . a baby with a soft penis. The first time I met him . . . and this was strange . . . he was at a party and his "date" was his mother. His mother still tries to dominate him . . . sometimes. . . . The things she does . . . she makes our life together intolerable. For me, there is no sex problem, there is only a mother problem. But I know I can never say to John what I see so plainly about his mother. It would be too painful for him. He would never accept ... and I would never say ... to bring it up would only drive us farther apart.

John sees his trouble as his own, having nothing to do with any woman: his body doesn't work. That's all. He knows for sure, because there are certain things he's never told anyone.

> I've tried things. I went to a very expensive prostitute. My body ... my lack of erections seem to get worse every year. I used to wake up with erections, but I almost never do now. I used to get erections ... when my first wife wasn't around ... now, when I masturbate I get partial erections ... little erections ... never a full erection for years ... maybe I'm too old now.

Impotence brings forth high emotions and confusion. Nearly everything John or Hilde says has the same hidden message: "Don't expect me to take any action that would restore those erections."

Two more reasons to do nothing. He thinks it's physical. She thinks it's psychological. They're both wrong. John's got the kind of impotence that most men get at some time in their lives. It comes neither from his body nor from his emotions. It's culturally induced. Some men are more susceptible than others—John is susceptible.

At the time his impotence first developed, John and his first wife could have cured it easily at home by changing what they did in bed only slightly. But John panicked. He turned his problem—which should have been temporary—into a severe condition that has continued for years. Now, John's severe impotence is still curable—but John and Hilde will need to make greater changes in their way of making love.

They haven't changed because they think impotence is hopeless.

John and Hilde are so concerned with keeping their secrets about that very emotional subject—his erections—that they of course never think to ask the questions that would let them know how severe a problem John actually has:

When *does* John get erections?
How much of an erection does he get?
How does he bring himself to orgasm?

Where does he want a woman to touch him?
How does he want a woman to touch him?

Too personal. The answers are too personal, according to John. And he doesn't *know* how or where he wants Hilde to touch him—exactly. And besides, he believes the answers wouldn't do any good. So does Hilde. She believes nothing will ever help John to get an erection.

> John has never in his whole life felt like me. I have seen him for two and a half years. *I know he can't have regular intercourse and never an orgasm. He's impotent.*

Hilde sees John's problem as absolute. He's impotent. His penis is dead. Hilde believes this because she is innocent. And it's not her fault. Too many men have lied to her.

But it's a wrong belief. A devastatingly harmful wrong belief. Every human's sexuality comes from all the sensory channels in the whole body. The erection is a *reaction*. The man without an erection is still a powerful sexual creature. *John is much closer in sexual behavior to Hilde's other lovers than she can imagine.*

Based on her experience of men, what she has seen and what they have told her, Hilde makes a very big mistake. She divides men into two groups: men who never get erections and men who always get erections.

Wrong division.

Erections don't work that way.

Facts About Getting Erections

Impotent Men Get Erections

John gets erections. Every day. Hilde believes he never gets erections because she never sees him get an erection and because he tells her he never gets an erection. He lies. All *healthy* men get erections. They have to. Erections are a natural body process like a heartbeat. The autonomic nervous system controls the erection, so the erection process goes on with no action from the man. Whether or not a man labels himself impotent, he gets erections four to six times a night while he sleeps.

Without John's doing anything except being a moderately healthy forty-six-year-old man, while he sleeps his body forces his penis erect. John—like many impotent men—also gets erections when he masturbates. And he gets erections in some situations with some women—at the beginning of his marriage with his first wife. Other impotent men get erections as long as they keep their pants on, some get erections during oral sex.

Secrets again. John gets erections, but he never lets his wife know. Okay, he is unaware of the erections he gets all night, but he does know he sometimes wakes up with an erection—which typically disappears the second he thinks of sex. He does know about the erections he gets when he masturbates, and the erections he used to get with his first wife. However, since he can't possibly use any of these erections to have penis-in-the-vagina intercourse with Hilde, he doesn't count them as "real" erections and he doesn't tell her.

Hilde is set on accepting the inevitable hopelessness of her husband's impotence, so she no longer looks at what actually happens to him or listens to what he tells her happens. She thinks he lies—even when he doesn't.

> He says he had an orgasm before he met me, but I can't imagine this. He also said that before we met he played with himself. But I don't believe him. I mean, I don't believe anything happened. I think when I play with him his thoughts are on his computer business or on the newspaper. He is just relaxing, like a little baby. [Hilde smiles.] I like him.

A dangerous secret. Like many impotent men, feeling his erections are his own business and are too personal and embarrassing to go into, John has presented Hilde with a picture of a man hopelessly damaged. With love, she accepts.

Impasse.

Every Man Loses His Erections

Every man loses his erections and every man lies. Hilde's first husband and then her lover led her to believe they always got erections. They lied. Any man who says he always get erections any time he wants them is lying. That is biologically impossible.

Facts:

Men are *supposed* to lose their erections.
All men lose their erections.
It is *normal* to lose your erection.

> *Question:* If all men lose their erections all the time, why don't women know this?
> *Answer:* Men are culturally pressured to lie.

Hilde:
> My first husband never in his life lost his erection. That man *thinks* sex and his penis goes straight up in the air.

Her first husband tells a different story:
> Most of the time when I can't get an erection, it doesn't worry me too much. It's one night—and then I'm fine. Sometimes it lasts for a couple days. Once or twice with Hilde I couldn't get an erection for several weeks. That got to me. I was starting to worry.

How can a man go for days or weeks—without his lover's realizing he is having trouble getting an erection?
"No trick, really," says the man. "Mostly my erection difficulties only last a few hours, a day or two at the most, so I engineer the situation to avoid close contact." "Once," he says with pride, "I maneuvered Hilde about in certain ways so that we didn't have sex for two weeks—and she never caught on that she was being maneuvered. She," he boasts, "thought she was the one who was avoiding sex."
How does he manage this?
Without much thought. Her lover has always concealed his erection

losses from women. He has done this for so long and so automatically that he no longer thinks of what he does as a lie—it's "just what a man does."

What a man will do to avoid telling a woman that his penis cannot always get hard:

1. *Pick a fight.* This is a favorite. "I get her mad so she *wants* me to stay away from her."
2. *Set up rules that the two of you will have sex only when he suggests it.* The man who says, "Sexually aggressive women turn me off," may really be saying, "I am scared that someday you will say you want to have sex at a time when I may feel unable to get an erection. I never want to take that chance so I think it's best if we have sex only *when* I want and *for as long* as I want and *in the way* that I want.
3. *Stop kissing and hugging you.* Before you suspect that he is having an affair, or that he doesn't love you anymore, you should first suspect that he is worried about losing his erection. As a man's fears increase, he will do fewer acts that might possibly lead to you wanting to have intercourse.
4. *Pretend he does not recognize your advances because he is too busy, doing important things or he is already asleep.* The truly fearful lover may even *arrange to sleep in different places or to go to bed on different schedules.*

Hundreds of lies to cover a biological certainty—like breathing. But all men lose their erections. That's the way the male body works.

The blood-flow crisis. Erections are caused by blood flow. You have to know that simple biological fact. When John sleeps, his autonomic nervous system triggers his blood to flow into his penis—automatically during the stages of sleep called rapid-eye-movement sleep. Occasionally when a man is awake he will also get one of these pure body-function erections. However, the erections that separate the impotent men from other men are the erections he gets when he is awake and with a woman to whom he wants to make love. Those erections are triggered by erotic arousal. While John's conscious body reacts to his arousal, the level of that arousal is too low. If he did build his arousal high enough, he would get an erection. In the heat of passion, his blood would rush into three tubelike areas inside his penis, where it would stay trapped. Erection.

Blood flow is variable. A man's erection is slightly bigger one day and slightly smaller the next because the total amount of blood running through his whole body varies slightly from day to day. So we have a culture in which a man feels pressured to have his biggest erection every time he makes love. But his animal body, paying no attention to cultural expectations, sends blood to his penis in relation to the total blood volume in his body—which varies from day to day.

On top of that, blood flow to the penis is powerfully influenced by what a man does when he makes love. If John becomes erotically close to Hilde his blood will rush into his genitals. John never gets close. He stays away, concentrates on his anxiety about his failure. His anxiety makes his arousal go down, his blood is diverted away, and he never gets an erection.

Every man loses his erection the same way: something lowers his arousal so that his blood eases out of his penis. John, who hasn't had penis-in-the-vagina intercourse for five years, and Hilde's first husband have the same male body—and at any moment of erection loss they go through the same biological process. And so does every man.

Erections are tricky. They go up and down while you make love. At any given time you can be in a situation where keeping your arousal high enough is nearly impossible.

Simple loss of erection happens all the time. No matter. It's *temporary.* Change the circumstances, the arousal goes up. Here's the crucial part: it's no problem if you do the right things. To do the right things you have to recognize what *caused* the temporary erection loss. If you've had too many drinks, sober up. If you are exhausted, get some sleep. If it's medication, consult a physician about changing it or reducing the dose. If it's the pressure of parents, stay somewhere else. If you are under work pressure, expect difficulty and take the low arousal in stride. Change your expectations till the work situation changes.

Impotence develops, in many cases, because, like John, many men have unreasonable expectations. An erect penis is simply one with good blood flow and shows that a man is physically fit, rested, peaceful, relaxed, and getting enough of the erotic touch he likes best.

Instead, many men—and women—believe that a real man *always* gets a hard-on, and being sexually innocent, they believe the man with a stiff penis is more masculine than the next man, more virile and sexier.

Wrong belief.

It's only a sign that we live in the sexual dark ages that we teach males to take great pride in a part of their biology that happens naturally if they don't do anything to stop it. A male who mistakenly begins to care about whether he has three-quarters as much blood one time and eight-ninths as much blood the next time, a male who believes such differences are significant and have something to do with him personally, may be headed for trouble.

Variability is a different concept. Few of us want to be bothered thinking about anything that changes every time it happens. And so it is with erections; we ignore what actually happens and what actual steps can be taken to maintain erections. Having a great desire for a simple yes or no answer to erection, we make up a simple yes or no answer.

However, in the case of erections there is no simple yes or no. Blood flow is never completely solid and it never completely stops. With blood flow there is only variability.

The Three Causes of Erection Failure: Biology, Biology, and Biology

Only three things stop blood flow:

1. Anxiety
2. Insufficient eroticism
3. Body failure

All erection loss is biological. Your body is geared naturally to send enough blood to your penis to make it erect. Whenever that fails to happen, something has interfered with your biology. If your body is interfering, if your body doesn't work, you have a purely *physical impotence.* If you are interfering, if your anxiety or your inadequate lovemaking blocks your blood flow, then it is your behavior that is causing your impotence. You are like most men. You have *behavioral impotence.*

Physical Impotence: What to Do About It?

Most men are convinced that if they can't get erections there is something seriously wrong with their penises. Like John. John believes his is a biological problem. He's believed this for years. Just believed without ever knowing how to find out. But there's a very simple test to find out.

The Abel Scale: Six Questions to Help You Decide If You Have Physical Impotence*

Ask yourself these six questions *exactly* the way they are worded. Three or more *yes* answers indicate the need for a physical evaluation by an impotence specialist.

1. I always get less than a full, 100 percent erection.   yes   no
2. I never have full, 100% erections on awakening in the morning or awakening during the night.   yes   no
3. It frequently or always takes me longer to ejaculate than it used to.   yes   no
4. I always get less than a full, 100 percent erection during masturbation or oral sex.   yes   no
5. I frequently or always ejaculate a smaller amount than I used to.   yes   no
6. I rarely or never have premature ejaculation.   yes   no

* Developed by Gene G. Abel, M.D., and a team of researchers at the Department of Psychiatry, College of Physicians and Surgeons, Columbia University, the Abel Scale was devised by measuring the answers to eighteen questions routinely used to differentiate physical from behavioral impotence against the night erections. The subjects were sixty diabetic men, whose answers were recorded by a polygraph on successive nights in a sleep lab. Of the eighteen questions, these six were found to differentiate pure body failure from behavioral interference.

The study was supported by grant AM25630 (awarded to the authors by the National Institute of Arthritis, Metabolism and Digestive Disease), NIH grant RR00645, and NIH grant MH 30906.

John answers yes to questions 1 and 4. Two yes answers aren't enough. He fails to have physical impotence. If John had answered yes to more than two questions, he might still be free of physical impairment, but he should have an evaluation by a physician or multidisciplinary team capable of checking his nerve conduction, hormone levels, penile blood pressure, and, most important, the presence of his natural sleep erections.

Measuring Your Natural Sleep Erections

There are simple devices a man can wear to record his own erection measures while he sleeps in his own bed. Or he could sleep several nights in a hospital, hooked to a polygraph, which would trace out the size of his sleep erections. Or he could take a new test developed by a French physician to measure rigidity.

If a man did measure his sleep erections, what could he expect to find out? Of the men who believe they are totally physically impotent and pursue the matter far enough to measure their nighttime erections, more than 70 percent find that they are physically perfect.

Three Vital Steps Before Surgery

The usual finding in the fewer than 30 percent of men with physical impotence is that they have "some" physical impairment.

Which brings us to the essence of the physical problem: Because we are talking about blood flow affected by what a man does in bed with his lover, a man doesn't know how much of his erection failure comes from his body and how much comes from the way he makes love—and no physician can tell him. Most impotent men stop touching their lovers. They withdraw. And so by the time their physical problem is diagnosed, their lovemaking skills have diminished so much that they also have a behavioral problem.

Because all men are powerfully affected by erotic touch, the only way a man with some impairment can find out exactly how much of an erection he can get without surgery is to build his lovemaking skills to the highest possible level and see how much of an erection he gets. His first step should be to do what behaviorally impotent men do: follow the Ten-Day Plan.

A physically impaired impotent man *should* consider a surgical remedy but only *after* he has: 1. determined whether his physical problem is temporary; 2. sharpened his lovemaking skills enough to find out if he is one of the group of physically impotent men who—through heightened eroticism—are able to regain erections that might have been thought medically impossible; 3. sharpened his lovemaking skills to such an extent that *he and his lover* feel comfortable using the surgically implanted or repaired erection, since surgery cannot restore lost lovemaking skills.

Behavioral Impotence: How It Works

This impotence is the kind a surgeon can do nothing about. It is the kind most men have. It is the kind of impotence John has. And John reacts to the news of his perfect health the way most impotent men react: the discovery upsets him. Lacking a specific physical source, John assumes that he has a serious psychological problem. Maybe he's crazy.

Wrong assumption.

Unfortunately, behavioral impotence has been labeled psychological. Wrong label.

There are no psychological causes of impotence. Impotence caused by anxiety or insufficient erotic stimulation while you are making love to a woman has little to do with emotional disturbance or deep-seated conflicts. Rather than setting one man apart from another as psychological problems do, *the problem of behavioral impotence happens to nearly every man at some time in his life.* And unlike problems caused by powerful psychological forces, most men can solve this problem with a very short course of the right things to do when they make love. Success rates for all impotent men who complete sex therapy are at 80 percent.

Rather than having a psychological trauma, like most men who become impotent, John had a temporary erection loss—and then he panicked. He made himself worse and went on doing the wrong things with no idea of how to do the right things.

Temporary erection loss happens in any of a thousand situations that happen to make a man anxious. John did get erections. Then he got into one of those situations that could be expected to cause complete loss of erection in any man.

Things were getting good in bed—then came my company's first merger. My mind was on the business twenty-four hours a day. I would take time out to be with Gail, but I always felt nervous. I felt I really shouldn't be with her. I should be working. It was fall. That September we had successful intercourse eight out of ten times we tried. The rest of the time—when I would lose my erection and fall out—we would just play around, sometimes have oral sex. In October I was able to have penetration only two out of ten times. And in November and December I was back to where I had started before I met Gail—no erections with a woman—ever.

John's erection loss should have been temporary. After the merger his work anxiety disappeared and when that happened, his erections should have flowed naturally along, except: John overreacted.

Erection Anxiety

John did the most dangerous thing a man can do: he became *anxious about his erection.* His new anxiety centered on: Am I going to get an erection? Will I ever get an erection again? Today, when I masturbated I got an erection, but was it a *full* erection? If I do get a full erection, will I be able to keep it? In September he had simple anxiety which was causing temporary loss of erection. By December he had erection anxiety. Erection anxiety causes long-term impotence because every time you make love—if you are anxious about that, about making love—you will block your own blood flow to your penis. And you can't get away. Once you link your anxiety to your erection you repeat your failures forever. Unless you do something to break your anxiety about your erection.

In the early months with his first wife, to correct his temporary erection loss he needed to raise his arousal. Instead, overcome with embarrassment, he hid the problem from his lover. He withdrew. No kissing, no hugging, no naked rolling around in the bed, no touching. John waited. He decided he must get an erection *before* he touched his lover.

Wrong decision.

Because he had withdrawn from touching Gail, he lost some of his skills. With fewer skills he got fewer erections. That made him anxious. And he found himself trapped: he got morning erections; he got masturbatory erections; but John felt—after failing and failing and failing again—that he might never get an erection with a woman.

Profile of the Impotent Man

All right, we have a situation in which *all* men *will* lose their erection. Given that situation can we predict the men who will become impotent? Yes.

The men who are most likely to have a *severe reaction* to that loss of erection—a reaction so severe that they anxiously block their own natural blood flow to their penises—share certain qualities:

They are conscientiously responsible.

They are used to making decisions for other people—including their lovers. They make decisions fast. They stick to their decisions.

They have a record of competence at controlling their environment.

They do not expect—or, perhaps, even like—other people to help them, even their lovers.

They keep their lovemaking confined within a certain narrow range.

And, though they love women, they *sometimes* feel, for one reason or another, that they must maintain a distance from the female sex.

Used to taking control, the impotent man fails to realize the issue is blood flow and he can't *make* his blood flow where he wants by direct action. By himself. By keeping a manly distance from the female sex.

Rather than a ninety-eight-pound weakling who lets other men kick sand in his face, the impotent man is much more likely to be aggressive, a success in his work, a man of principles and integrity, who cares about his lover's feelings. He is almost certainly a success by the standards of his culture. Which is exactly what gives some men such a high likelihood of having difficulty maintaining an erection. The skills men learn to become a success in this culture—taking charge, trying harder, making things work—are in direct conflict with the erotic skills one needs to get erections.

Every Man Past the Age of Forty

Young men of sixteen and twenty-two develop chronic bouts of erection failure, being susceptible to so many of the same initial causes that affect all men. But it is the man past forty, the man like John, who has an additional susceptibility. Not because, being past forty, he should become impotent. Healthy men *should* continue getting erections and making love as long as they are alive.

However, John, because he is past forty, has to face a few additional causes of *temporary* erection loss.

He no longer gets a number of inappropriate erections. True. Men past forty get fewer inappropriate erections.

During your baby days, your days of immaturity, you got thousands of inappropriate erections—erections useful for neither fathering a child nor making love. As a baby you got an erection at the slightest touch to your penis. As a twelve-year-old, a sixteen-year-old, you got an erection when you crossed your legs, you got an erection when you slid down a pole, often you got an erection seemingly unconnected with anything. Your young body was inappropriately overreactive.

Fortunately, as you pass twenty-five and then thirty-five your body begins to act appropriately. You get most of your erections by building your arousal.

The problem with this change is that most of your life you've been young, so you have very little perspective on what is natural for the man past forty. What do you do? Do you compare yourself with all other men your age? No. Or with yourself twenty years from now? No. Almost impossible. Because you and all the men your age and all the men twenty years older than you keep the news of their erections secret. Because of this, it's very easy for you to do the dangerous thing. You will compare you now with the you of your youth, getting all those inappropriate erections. Catastrophe. You get a distorted notion of what should be happening. You may become overanxious. Down goes your arousal. You may withdraw from building your arousal with a woman. Down goes your arousal. Then the natural thing follows. With such low arousal, you, of course, have trouble getting an erection. But you needn't have trouble. What is dangerous is your reaction.

The proper reaction would be to face the loss of what you never needed in the first place in a positive manner, as you faced the loss of your girlish voice, your hairless cheeks, and your formerly four-foot self. The loss of your inappropriate erections has no effect on your continued ability to get full erections with a woman—unless you react by *doing something* to lower your arousal.

Long separation from a lover can wreck havoc with the blood flow to your penis. Again, it is your *reaction* that changes the problem from a temporary inconvenience to a seemingly permanent condition. Breaking up, divorce, and death, all separate men from their lovers, and it is that *separation,* in and of itself, that can be practically guaranteed to make the man unable to maintain an erection when he initially tries to make love. At the time John first tried so anxiously to make love to Hilde—and succeeded only in sweating all over her—he had not been with a woman for two years.

Even though most of us have been led to believe making love is more natural than riding a bike—once you do it a few times you never forget—that isn't exactly so. We never forget about how to put the penis in the vagina, but we may well forget the thousands of erotic actions we can use to build our excitement so that putting the penis in the vagina becomes the easiest, most natural erotic act. Not only is that a learned skill, you also can't assume that, because you had the skill once and simply haven't used it for a long time, you still have it.

Men separated from their lovers because of illness or surgery are also susceptible to temporary impotence from loss of skill. But does a man in that circumstance tell himself the true story? Probably not. He probably feels certain that during surgery some nerve pathway has been damaged. He tells himself he was fine before this surgery, so it's obvious the surgery has left him impotent.

Men often conclude that a heart attack, pneumonia, hernia operation, or vasectomy has left them impotent.

Such a faulty conclusion is shared in some instances by very young men. The twenty-two-year-old victim of a motorcycle accident that left him with a broken pelvis, multiple fractures, and months of hospitalization will also have trouble reestablishing his erotic skills and will also believe absolutely in the accident as the cause of his impotence. However, it is the older man who is most susceptible.

- He has a greater likelihood of separation from his lover.
- He expects that because of his age his ability to get an erection is so fragile it may disappear.
- He is anxious about his natural loss of inappropriate erections.
- And he hides his erection anxieties from his lover.

Which is exactly why so many men over forty are impotent.

So here is John, forty-six and noticing he gets fewer inappropriate erections, coming out of a period of years of staying away from women, divorced once because he was impotent, lying to Hilde about the erections he does get, and having done all the wrong things, he has built his temporary erection loss into a major condition that has nearly ruined his personal life.

What could he have done to avoid the whole mess from the beginning?

At the beginning he could have taken the simplest cure. When he first transferred his work anxiety to erection anxiety he could have stopped his impotence right there.

How?

By following the First and Easiest Cure Ever for Behavioral Impotence.

The First and Easiest Cure Ever for Behavioral Impotence

Before men knew how to have a Freudian thought, they worried about their erections and lost them. Nearly two hundred years ago a clever physician discovered the secret of erection anxiety and published the basic treatment used by today's sex therapists. As 1786 was a less liberated time, the innovative Dr. John Hunter was roundly ignored for his great discovery.

No matter. Dr. Hunter was already famous for his discovery of the relationship between emotional stress and heart attacks and for his elite position as "surgeon extraordinary" to King George III, which may have prompted the good doctor to discover erection anxiety in the first place.

Circumstantial evidence indicates that King George III, in addition to losing certain colonies to the American revolutionaries, was tortured by bouts of impotence. Dr. Hunter, of course, concealed the name of his patient, but he reports spending an inordinate amount of time with a "gentleman," who certainly was of the right age, wealth, rank, and had the appropriate number of mistresses to be king. The "gentleman" presented himself to Dr. Hunter in quite an emotional state, claiming he had lost his "virility." He had called Dr. Hunter to his estates because the good doctor was quite clever and was not likely to repeat the nonsense about rhinoceros-horn powder mixed with wine that most medical practitioners were espousing in the 1780s. Dr. Hunter, who was known to observe physical mechanisms quite closely and objectively and to come to his own conclusions, had already made several important observations about sex.

> To perform this act well, the body should be in health and the mind should be perfectly confident of the powers of the body; the mind should have no difficulties, no fears, no apprehensions: *not even an anxiety to perform the act well* . . .

However, Dr. Hunter also warned: "When a man's anxiety about performing well" causes the mind to interfere with what is an involuntary action, "failure must be the consequence." He further observed that "every failure increases the evil" and noted that when anxiety interrupts the natural power of sexual functioning and when the victim does not know the "true cause of this interruption" he will lay the blame on the body.

Dr. Hunter's first task was to find out whether the overwrought gentleman's problem was purely in his body. Dr. Hunter could have played it safe and asked the seemingly appropriate questions which would have caused little embarrassment to himself or his important patient. He could have asked about the pressures of being an Englishman of such high rank right when the bloody colonists were seizing control of vast amounts of territory rightfully owned by the king of England. Or he could have become more involved in gossip, asking if the patient was upset because his esteemed wife objected to his mistresses. Or he could have asked if he hated his mother or women in general.

But, always a scientist, Dr. Hunter asked: When do you get erections? The gentleman continued to have full erections "at unnecessary times." Yes, the "natural power" was still there.

Dr. Hunter's next question was a bit unexpected: Did the patient have this problem with every woman? No, he was continuing to make love to several women "as well as ever." In fact, the gentleman lost his erection with only one woman. Was she plain? Was she sexually less arousing? No. She was the very woman the gentleman most adored. The one woman he wanted to impress with his sexual performance.

Because he was so anxious to please this lover sexually, what happened to the gentleman is exactly what is likely to happen to you. Right at the time he should have been rapturously enjoying the sensual delights of the love of his life he "had a doubt or fear [which caused] his inability to perform the act."

Dr. Hunter's prescription:

> I told him that he might be cured, if he could perfectly rely on his own power of self-denial. . . . He told me that he could. I then told him that he was to go to bed with this woman, but first promise to himself that he would not have intercourse with her for six nights, let his inclinations and powers be what they would: which he engaged to do: and also to let me know the result.

The gentleman reported that soon after he went to his lover's bed knowing that he must not have intercourse, he got an erection. "Instead of going to bed with the fear of inability, he went with fears that he should be possessed of too much desire." This happened, and he wished he could shorten the time, but dutifully continued to carouse with his lover without using his erection for the full six days. Then the gentleman broke his cycle of failure. He gained complete confidence. The problem vanished forever.

While the six-day miracle cure seems at first glance too simplistic to really restore erections except on one long-dead Englishman of high rank

92

and many mistresses, the cure *does* work. The male body functions essentially the same, regardless of the male in the body. If the man rids himself of erection anxiety *and* increases erotic contact he gets an erection.

To tell any man with erection anxiety to stop being anxious about his erections is useless. Dr. John Hunter knew this.

How He Fails to Restore His Erections

At one time or another Gail told John not to worry, Hilde told John not to worry, even John used to tell himself not to worry.

Impossible.

There is only one way to stop erection anxiety: become an excellent lover without using your erection.

John could have been cured five years ago by doing nothing more than carousing erotically with Gail for a week without penetration. Such a thought never crossed his sexually primitive mind. Like a marooned swimmer who beats the water so hard he drowns in his own waves, aggressive John follows the dark-ages wisdom that a man's first job is to get it up and keep it up. He decides to make his penis work the same way he has conquered his business problems: by sheer force of will. He will attack the problem of his limp penis *directly*. Unfortunately, this never works because erections occur *indirectly*. They occur when you dream of making love. They occur when you *raise your arousal*. Working to make yourself get an erection *lowers your arousal*. Every direct attempt frustrates the man's natural biology and increases anxiety. Anxiety blocks arousal. Blocked arousal stops blood flow. Taking this route, John has to fail. But John doesn't know this. And so, using his primitive common sense, he decides to fix his broken penis himself using the secret home remedies that have led more than one man into trauma.

He Tries to Cure Himself: The Five Worst Mistakes a Man Can Make

1. I'll Do This Alone

"I feel like I want to solve this thing by myself. It's my problem and I've got to solve it on my own," says John, echoing the most typical reaction of impotent men.

However, *on his own,* John has no erection problem. All night when he sleeps, he gets erections. When he touches his own penis he gets a partial erection and always an orgasm; he *knows* exactly how to touch his own genitals to come to orgasm. His problem is getting an erection *with* his lover.

2. The Search for the Right Woman

John—like many men—counts on *just looking* at a naked woman to restore his erection. As the months go by and his own anxiety leads him to get fewer and fewer erections, he mistakenly concludes that his problem may be Gail—perhaps she isn't sexy enough for him. John clings to the American schoolboy myth that there is a woman out there whose breasts are so big or whose fingernails are painted so red or whose pubis is so perfect that one look—Wham! and his penis will stiffen.

However each time he meets a woman he keeps all his sexual secrets to himself. He barely touches her; he won't let her touch him. And naturally what follows is low arousal—too low to send his blood rushing into his penis.

3. The Rod-and-Piston Approach

John is obsessed with his "cock." "I know I should get my mind off it," he says. "I know it. But there it is—all I think about is 'Cock, cock, cock, cock.'" Because he believes in the hydraulic principle of the penis—that this part of his body is simply a rod and piston going up and down with no connection to how comfortable he feels with a woman or what he does when he makes love to her—he concentrates all his energy on fixing his erection. Directly. He wills himself to try harder.

Trying harder doesn't work. Every time he pressures himself to get an erection he lowers his arousal. There is no way to pressure a reflex.

John wants his erection working *before* he tells a woman exactly how to touch him. Which is fine for him to want. However, his biology is stubbornly consistent. It always works the same way—increased arousal, then reflex. John can wish to reflex first—and then increase his arousal, he can swear to the stars that this is what he will do. Still, his body will not budge. The body—always the same—always waits. Increased arousal—then erection.

Impasse.

4. Compulsive Repetition

John cannot, for the life of him, understand why his body is doing this. "Why is this happening to me?" he asks. And yet, he *makes* it happen time after time—by *compulsive repetition.*

He wants to get his erections going again—and he wants to keep his distance from women. Impossible. But he wants this *so* desperately that even though what he does fails every time, he keeps repeating it. He assumes the role of a male stud whose job is to get an erection, penetrate, get her an orgasm, get him an orgasm, and get out. He assumes this role with all women, even with women who would never want him in that role.

5. I'll Stay Away from Women Altogether

So much failure astounds John. It's intolerable. He is a man who succeeds. He expects to succeed at everything. With no help from anybody. "If I can't do it well," he tells himself, "I won't do it." Secretly he waits for a spontaneous cure. "After I'm over this impotence thing," he says, "then I'll get close to my wife." While he is waiting his first wife leaves him. Years go by. He meets Hilde. He soaks the sheets. He worries. He calms down. He modifies. He now says, "If I can't do it well, I'll do it less." John and Hilde have sex once a week. He holds himself a bit apart, still waiting for the spontaneous cure.

No chance. The longer he avoids letting a woman know what excites him the further away he gets from being able to easily have erections with women. As the days and years go by, he loses some of the sexual skills he once had.

Choosing the Worst Kind of Lovers

The sexual skills to overcome impotence are not exclusively male. They are possessed by the couple. Which means any woman can teach a willing man how to get erections. Unfortunately, the independent, aggressive man who prefers to keep his distance from women also prefers distant women. And so, he chooses the worst kind of lover for an impotent man.

The Sex Object

She's just a little thing. Five foot one. With big round breasts, firm as a girl's. Pretty little legs. A luscious ass. Years ago, when I was still married to Gail, I would see Carol every now and then. I would put my hands all over that juicy ass. And she would give it to me. We saw each other off and on for two years. I tell you, we were never together when we didn't have sex. She would let me do anything to her. Anything I wanted.

Remembering only how exciting this used to be for him—the secret affair, the willing woman, those "great round breasts" and the "juicy ass"—and innocent of certain facts such as: he never saw her when he was pressured by business, only on his lark days; he hasn't seen her since he developed erection anxiety—John has a new thought.

It might not be me, John tells himself, after his try at "everything" with Gail fails. Maybe Gail isn't sexy enough, maybe if I was with a *really* sexy woman, he says, thinking of Carol, the classic sex object who started "putting out" when she was a high-school cheerleader.

At the age of forty-two and still "putting out," she has more one-night stands than she can count. What the sex object does, of course, has nothing to do with *giving* a man anything. What Carol does is lie down passively and allow the man to give her his penis any way he would like to give her his penis. As John says, "She gave me everything. She would just lie there."

Carol is the first woman he tries to have sex with after he has trouble getting erections. He hopes that she will be so sexy . . . his "cock will just shoot up." Seeing that he can't get an erection, Carol turns into a definitely unsexy woman. She screams. She curses. She is so angry, she is ready to kill him. "How dare you do this to me? You goddamned bastard. What are you trying to pull?" With her rage, she reveals the other side of the woman who makes herself into a sex object: she sees men as big dicks. From their first time together Carol always treated John as though the only important thing about him was his rigid penis—and when he tries to approach her without this prize possession she panics. Sexually, she knows how to do one thing: "lie there." Having nothing to offer a man without an erection, Carol gets furious.

Carol is the worst of the worst lovers for a man with erection anxiety. She is a penis checker. Her sexual self-image is bound up in *his erection.* "Why are you doing this to *me?*" she screams, completely uninterested in his anxieties or his sexual needs. She curses because she's threatened. She expects men to get erections just because she takes her clothes off. Being the counterpart of the macho man, the sex object also subscribes to the fallacious "perfect tits" theory of male sexual arousal. Secretly, she believes that if her breasts were young enough, firm enough, sexy enough, John *would have to* get an erection. Deep inside she fears that perhaps her breasts aren't that great anymore, maybe she isn't that sexy anymore.

She says she knows she's sexy. However, she curses at the limp penis that sends her the message "I don't find you attractive."

It's the wrong message.

John does find her terribly arousing. But in keeping with his lifelong approach to women, he never tells her. He never lets her touch him, other than a hug or a kiss. He never touches her, except to put his erect penis in and take it out. But for his penis to erect, he has to raise his arousal. The old pattern isn't enough now. Her screaming makes his erection anxiety worse. Keeps him away so he can't raise his arousal.

The Prostitute

Unable to give up his idea that just looking at the right woman will cure him, John goes in search of the "Oriental Express." He's picked up the idea somewhere that a really good prostitute may know things other women don't, may have some fabulous trick to help him get an erection.

Wrong idea.

According to John's report, the high-priced prostitute *is* beautiful. Her black shiny hair hangs below her waistline, her breasts are exquisite, her legs are long and lithe, and her face is perfect. Almond eyes show her Chinese heritage, her lightly painted mouth is sensual, her teeth are small and straight, her skin is perfectly white. She is willing to do anything he wants. She will put his penis down her throat. She will dress in leather. She will urinate on his toes. All he has to do is name it and he's got it. And so, there he is, there she is, and there is nothing in all the world for John to do but get it up. He can't read a newspaper. He can't take a hot shower. Or talk about the opera. He's afraid to touch her. The pressure to get an erection is really on. His anxiety goes up, up, up. No chance for an erection. This situation is much too stressful for an impotent man.

After some difficult moments for John, she offers fellatio, but he's too embarrassed, and so anxious that he knows the truth: under these circumstances there is "no way I can get it up."

Innocent of his biology as ever, John misinterprets his experience:

"It was then," he says, "that I *knew* I was in trouble. When I saw that gorgeous woman's body, those perfect breasts, that long black hair, and nothing happened, I knew I was in deep trouble."

Wrong expectation.

Just looking may have worked when he was sixteen, but so did crossing his legs, and so did many random occurrences that had very little to do with erotic skills. Just looking is, in fact, one of the least effective ways a man can build his arousal. Sight, sound, smell, taste, fantasy, and touch will all build arousal. Combinations build the most arousal. However, the single most powerful sensual path to erotic arousal is touch. John shies away from touch.

The Woman Who Cheers You On

"Don't worry about your erection," said his first wife, suggesting a feat far beyond her erection-obsessed husband's capabilities. "You know why we can solve this?" she said with assurance. "Because we are in love. Being in love *means* you can overcome anything if you try hard enough."

Unknown to his young and eager bride, John's blood flow is triggered by his autonomic nervous system which works on the relaxation principle. When he's asleep and unable to try at all, he gets erection after erection.

His first wife—a go-getter like her husband—felt that the obvious answer was for the two of them to be sexier. Gail's version of sexier overlooked loving touch and went straight on to kinky.

Gail creates situations that push her sexually anxious husband to give the stud performance of his life. Faced with an impotent husband, gogetter Gail does the worst possible thing: she dresses up.

> We had just moved out away from the city. The place was all unpacked boxes. And when I got home I was a bit irritated that she hadn't gotten farther on with it—I remember that . . . and I heard this voice—it was Gail, but strange—from the bedroom. I thought, perhaps, something had happened. I pushed open the door—the bedroom was in perfect order . . . and there she stood . . . in red underwear. The brassiere had holes in the middle for the nipples to come through. She wore a red garter belt with no panties. She had on boots—black leather—way up over her knees. I had seen her body many times—but this was different. It was exciting. Only nothing happened. I didn't get an erection. She had . . . well, she tied me up. She spanked me. I think she was disappointed . . . I mean, when I didn't get an erection.
>
> And then she suggested . . . well, we went to one of those erotic motels. The ones with the mirrors on the ceilings and it had a waterbed and a fur bedspread and a big screen with dirty movies and they . . . you know the drawer where they usually have the Gideon Bible . . . this place had a vibrator with eight attachments. She really liked the place. She had a little suitcase full of scotch. We were joking about her getting me drunk and taking advantage of me . . . and then she gave a toast. "If this doesn't do it, John baby, nothing will." It didn't do it and I think she gave up on me after that.

Wrong expectation.

Gail had dragged her poor husband to the worst possible place for an impotent man—to a place that screamed Perform! Like many impotent men who had been dragged off to erotic motels before him, John was, of course, unable to adapt to the super expectancy that he would feel quickly aroused and he was even more depressed by his failure. It was then that he classified himself absolutely hopeless. Even here, he says to himself, with *"everything"* to turn me on, with men in room after room on all sides of me using their giant erections to screw for hours, here I am—a hopeless failure.

In that room with the mirrors I had the impression that my penis withdrew into itself—actually shriveled.

Gail's theory: If regular sex doesn't work, kinky sex will. The irony is that Gail—as she told friends later—didn't really *want* to do "kinky" stuff. Shedding all responsibility, she told her friends and retold her friends: "We tried everything."

"Everything," one should note, did not include either reducing John's erection anxiety or touching him in the ways that he would find erotically exciting. But then both Gail and John had no way of knowing that this would help them.

Status quo: low arousal, no erection. When Gail finally leaves John they are both sad and somewhat relieved.

The Lady Who Says, "It's All in Your Head"

"You have a small erection, then you get cerebral about it. That computer in your head starts working," says Hilde, "and your erection disappears." Living in the age where people search for a psychological cause for everything, Hilde pins her husband's failure on his mother.

It's his mother. My husband has to break the dependency. When we were dating, she would only allow him to see me one night a week. Her forty-two-year-old son she allowed one date a week. She would call my house an hour after he arrived asking when he would be coming home. One time I said tomorrow and she screamed. Screamed and threatened suicide. Now she calls every day. She will never speak to me when I am alone with her. She barely speaks when I am with John. She spent ten days in our home and you could write on a postcard the number of sentences she said.

As far as sex goes, I am satisfied. I get what I want. For me there is no sexual problem, there is only a mother problem.

Having compiled very strong evidence, Hilde believes that his somewhat unusual closeness with his mother has left John in a sexually child-like state. Although she feels sure that, if she can get him to break the "intellectual and emotional dependency" on his mother, his "soft penis" will disappear, she also feels this subject is one that could never be mentioned directly to John. So she chooses a path of "small acts of sabotage" to break the mother-son relationship.

To those who follow the psychology of human interaction in the popular media her hypothesis of cause and effect sounds good because it sounds so familiar. The only trouble with pinning the responsibility of what John does in bed on his mother is that his mother is never in bed with him.

His mother's part in her son's becoming sexually anxious was much less dark and mysterious than Hilde believes. Her role was simple: she kept her son away from females. Because his mother kept him away from females as long as she could, John was always slightly tense with women. By the time he started having sexual play with his first wife, John had had much less practice than other men his age, which led him to do very little with her erotically and so his body always received fairly low erotic stimulus. Because of that, his erections were always a bit less dependable than the next guy's. John failed to build the skills that would give him lifelong sexual confidence.

At this late date, even if he had a conflict with his mother to resolve, he also has a history of hundreds of erection failures with women. He has erection anxiety. He has erotic inhibitions with lovers. His mother dependency may have contributed to his problems—years ago. But now even if he spends several years successfully working out this mother-dependency issue, he still has to go to bed with Hilde. And when he licks her naked breasts, he will still worry about his penis becoming erect. And because of his numerous real-life failures, he will still be shy of touching a woman. His mother cannot help him with this, but his lover can. And Hilde does.

Doing the Right Things: Five Steps to Getting an Erection

He kisses her breasts. He rubs his warm, soft penis against her clitoris until she orgasms. They repeat this limited sex act once every week. It's as though their erotic love is a path that should be twenty feet wide and he has decided to walk on a one-foot-wide section of the path. He has made the path very narrow. Hilde has joined him there. Now they have to change.

The goal: a sex life with every erotic option—including erections.

An impotent man is unable to move *directly* to having an erection and penetrating, thrusting, and ejaculating. Any attempts to move directly to intercourse have to fail. Which is why so many people say impotence is hopeless: it is, *if* the impotent man tries to go *directly* to penis-in-the-vagina intercourse. John—like any severely impotent man—must move *indirectly,* going from one small step to the next.

A man who has developed erection anxiety *and* a complex secret way of touching his penis to bring himself to orgasm *and* inhibitions about being touched and touching, such a man who has such a long history of failure—a man like John, who appears to himself and his wife as a hopeless case—needs more than six nights carousing with a woman without using his erection. He needs to follow all of the five steps that conquer impotence:

1. Become an excellent lover without using your erection.
2. Touch his whole body/Touch her whole body.
3. Let your lover take responsibility for your erotic success.
4. Learn to feel comfortable losing your erection in front of a woman.
5. Stop trying harder. Learn to recognize the pattern that makes you want to try harder to keep your erection. Disrupt the pattern.

Each of these steps raises a man's arousal. Once his arousal goes high enough, a man *will* get an erection. That's all John has to do: raise his arousal. Either by reducing anxiety (which raises a man's arousal) or by increasing eroticism (which raises a man's arousal). If, like John, you need all five steps, use all five steps. However, there are gradations of impotence; a less severe problem needs less intervention. A man who worries about getting an erection sometimes may be able to solve his problem by doing no more than following step 5—or step 1. A man who fails 30 percent of the time may reduce his failure rate to 2 percent by following the first three steps. Which you will notice are the basic ways of generating desire discussed earlier.

The erotic body is exquisitely simple. What we are talking about is something more basic than restoring erections. We are talking about raising arousal. Because this is essential for all lovers, because the fullness of the lovers' erotic delight depends on this. The man—or woman—whose only wish is to be the best lover may just be clever enough to follow all five steps.

Say you are impotent, say you do master the five steps and cure yourself—if after a few years, you have a relapse, what then? Repeat the steps.

Becoming an Excellent Lover Without Using Your Erection

The first step is the most important: Become an excellent lover without using your erection. Should your erection reappear, *you must not use it. If you are unable to follow this step, nothing else you do makes any difference.*

John finds this rule ironic:
> If there's one thing Hilde and I are really good at, it's making love without my erection.

Not true. Although they have adapted to making love without John's having an erection, they have never *planned* to make love without his erection. They have never forbidden themselves to use his erection.

There's a decided difference between accepting no erection and forbidding yourself to use your erection. While he accepts the probability that his penis will remain soft *every single time he ever makes love,* John secretly hopes that "maybe this time I'll get hard." Every time he touches Hilde, he's thinking: Will I? Won't I? Those questions cause erection anxiety. So every time he has made love—for the past five years—he has kept his erection anxiety at the center of each experience. First step: Give up on the erection. Forbid yourself to use it. Make your erection beside the point. Let go.

Whole Body Touch

Touch is the most erotically powerful of all our senses. Following step 2, John is to: touch his whole body, touch her whole body. Divide the body—arms and hands, legs and feet, torso, head and neck, genitals. One lover touches, one lover is touched. For half an hour. Follow the sequence of the Ten-Day Plan, stretching the time into ten weeks. Explore one part of each lover's body each week until both lovers share a list of what each finds pleasurable.

As he concentrates on the erotic sensitivity of each part of his body and of each part of her body—forbidding himself to use any erection that should appear—John's erections will begin to come and go in their natural way. That's the plan. It always works. Except John can't do it. He and Hilde feel strange touching just the arms or just the legs with no intention of either of them having an orgasm—so, like most impotent couples, they act out their reluctance to change their sexual behavior by presenting—

The Impotent Couple's Usual Reasons for Staying That Way

- We don't have time.
  Impotent couples reduce the amount of time they spend having sex or stop altogether, so they are no longer used to making time. Besides, sexual interactions are associated with failure, so naturally they want to avoid them.

- Doing this isn't natural.
  Sex is no good if it isn't spontaneous.

The impotent couple feels that the steps are unnatural. But having sex the "natural" way the couple is impotent. The steps are designed to restructure a man's sex behavior so he can establish a *new* pattern of getting healthy, natural erections.

- We like *all* touching. We like everything.
  These are the words of a couple who are unable to *discriminate* one erotic touch from another. Erotic pleasure comes from discrimination.

- Touching by itself will never give me an erection.
  Impotent men believe this. That's why they spend years doing everything to cure themselves—except letting a woman touch them.

- But we want to have orgasms.
  Going for the goal of orgasm with every sexual interaction keeps an impotent man from getting erections again.

- But we know all this.
  Very unlikely. Most impotent couples reduce the number of times they have sex and reduce the number of touches they give each other. Most have no idea of which touch they would prefer—behind their knees or between their fingers or on their toes. Virtually none of the couples know what touch they prefer at different levels of arousal.

- It's silly.
  It's also silly to be healthy and suppress your erections.

Consider: *If* a man and woman have all the time in the world for sex, if they feel it's natural to erotically caress each other's body without touching the genitals, if they easily discriminate one erotic touch from another, if they believe that it is touching that leads to the greatest arousal, if they regularly experience erotic ecstasy without a thought of having an orgasm, if they possess the minutest knowledge of every erotic touch their lover wants and can change that touch as their lover's body changes from day to day and hour to hour—then the man would be getting erections. It should take you only about a minute to consider this. Which is certainly all the time you need to spend on the "reasons" to delay doing the right thing. Leap over them. Start *doing* the Ten-Day Plan.

Ten Days to Erotic Discovery—Lover to Lover

Basic Instructions to Be Followed for All Ten Days

Caress one part of your lover's body to discover which touch is most erotic. Your lover is to do the same for you on alternate days.

Day 1: Touch your lover's arms and hands.

Day 2: Your lover touches your arms and hands.

Day 3: Touch your lover's legs and feet.

Day 4: Your lover touches your legs and feet.

Day 5: Touch your lover's head and body (excluding genitals).

Day 6: Your lover touches your head and body (excluding genitals).

Day 7: Touch your lover's genitals.

Day 8: Your lover touches your genitals.

Day 9: Discover which touch, positions, and movements your lover finds most erotic during penis-in-the-vagina intercourse.

Day 10: Your lover discovers which touch, positions, and movements you find most erotic during penis-in-the-vagina intercourse.

During the ten days of erotic discovery

Find out:

- When your lover wants to be caressed.
- With what accessories your lover would like to be caressed. In water? With oil? With perfumed soap? What smell? With music? On a fur rug?
- How your lover would like to be touched. With fingers? With whole hand? With two hands? With tongue? What combinations of touch? How much pressure? Soft? Rough? How his performances change at different levels of arousal.

Your role: Take care of your lover completely.

Your lover's role: Feel each erotic sensation, differentiate which ones are better.

Time: Half an hour.

Do:

- Give your lover many, many sensual options to choose from.
- Continue touching for the full half hour.

Don't:

> • Use your reflexes to have penis-in-the-vagina intercourse or orgasm before you have established a history of building your arousal so high your erections come and go naturally as you touch your lover.
>
> • Caress each other. You are not to caress your lover during *your* time to *be* caressed. You must use all your concentration to discover your own eroticism. Only that for half an hour.

Like most impotent couples, John and Hilde need more time to explore each other's bodies. That's okay. The time isn't important. It's the sequence. A couple with a history of problems might need to do one step each week—making the Ten-Day Plan into a Ten-Week Plan. The important thing is to touch—no matter how reluctantly or anxiously. Each man and woman discovers how to be more erotic by discovering his or her difficulties.

For John, just touching is difficult. Because he can't follow the third step to conquer impotence: let your lover take responsibility for your erotic success.

His Lover's Responsibility

On the first day he touches *her* arms and hands—and discovers seventeen different touches she prefers. Great. But when it is his turn to be touched he can't seem to find the time, he is too tired, and he feels this is silly. A week later, he still hasn't let her touch him and he says he doesn't see what touching his arm has to do with his penis. Two weeks later, when he finally lets her touch him, John comes up against the impotent man's essential difficulty.

A Man's Fears He Can't Tell a Woman

"I can't tell a woman my *inner thoughts.*" John says this to explain why after Hilde has spent nearly an hour caressing his arms and legs and another half hour caressing his legs and feet, she still knows nothing specific about how he likes to be touched. She has no list for him.

He knows, but he won't tell her. Instead, like many impotent men, he spends a great deal of time talking about how he doesn't like to be touched, how he has never liked to be touched, and how there is nothing a woman could do to learn how he would like to be touched. On the genitals, yes, a woman could touch him there, but she must stay away from the rest of his body.

When pressed for some small preference, John says:

> "Okay, when I think at all about her touch on my thighs, about the type of pressure, or the variability of motion, I would have to say I like a heavy pressing of her whole hand, followed by a light touch. It is that lighter touch with her fingertips that I find most erotic.
>
> I told Hilde that I liked her to touch my thighs. I didn't think to tell her *how* or *which way*. I don't know why I didn't tell her. I know this has always been the case—I find it very difficult to tell any woman my *inner* thoughts.

Asked to define inner thoughts, he speaks in an incredulous voice as though the definition should be obvious.

> You know—inner thoughts are thoughts that you just know you have to keep to yourself. For instance, if by telling this thought to a woman I would be revealing something very personal about myself—then that thought is one which I know I should keep to myself. I do not like to reveal myself to a woman—or to anybody.

John believes that this is his personal idiosyncrasy. It isn't. It is nearly universal among men with repeated erection failure, transcending race, creed, and class. A European banker, a black auto mechanic in the South, a big city professor, and a NASA engineer use the identical phrase: *inner thoughts.*

Each one thinks this inability to let a woman—or anybody—know what makes him feel good is his special difficulty. It is an almost primitive fear of those men who are raised to be strong, silent, aggressive, competitive creatures. Men learn that there are certain gentle, tender pleasures that are off-limits for them. And the man is afraid that if he does experience tender pleasures, he will weaken and then terrible things will happen to him.

- "You can't let a woman know too much, she'll take advantage."

- "She was asking, did I like this and did I like that, but I didn't fall for that."

- "Sex to me is my genitals and my hands and my mouth, that's okay. It's really my genitals. I don't think of the rest of my body as having anything to do with sex. It makes me nervous—her touching my arms and running her hands over my legs and asking me questions like I was a schoolboy."

- "I can have sexual pleasure, but not that kind of pleasure."

John sees absolute doom, should he reveal his inner thoughts:

My gut reaction is that if she knew I liked to feel her hands on my thighs in just this way, she would know I like to be treated like a baby. And I do not want her to treat me like a baby. I would hate that.

He has tapped into primitive feelings. Intellectually, he knows his fantasy that any revelations about how he likes to feel a woman's fingers lightly caressing his inner thighs will turn him into a baby is just that—a fantasy. John never said that what he feared *would* happen. He said, "I *feel* that she would think I was a baby . . . I *feel* that I am not allowed to have *that kind of pleasure.*"

John is caught. He is not the kind of man who feels comfortable getting sensually close to a woman. He actually fears telling her how to touch him. However, if she is to help him, she has to know.

Impasse.

John has already taken this route. He has been unable to tell a great number of women which touch makes him feel more erotic—and with every one of them he has failed to get an erection.

Telling a woman exactly how to touch him is a change. Naturally, John feels uncomfortable. He is terrible at revealing what he likes. After a lifetime with no practice, that's to be expected. However, desperate and finally willing to try anything, he and his lover persevere, and with some struggle he is able to identify specific touch and to tell his lover:

I like to feel your hand on my thighs, your whole hand, pressing hard, then your fingertips lightly.

I like to feel both of your hands on the back of my neck, lightly touching behind my ears—your fingers in my hair, as I get more excited, your fingers pulling my hair.

I like to feel your hands on the inside of my upper arm, your thumb touching very high under my arm and falling back.

I like to feel nothing on my calves or ankles—uninteresting.

I like to feel a heavy touch on my back, followed by the same light-finger touch that is so sexy on my thighs.

That's the major breakthrough. Once John can tell a lover which touch makes him feel good, he is beginning the process that will bring his erections back.

Touching His Genitals in a Series of Small Steps

The Ten-Day Plan rules apply to touching the genitals, with one variation: the lovers must slow down. They are to discover the better genital touch through a series of small steps. First small step: *John is to show Hilde how he touches his penis to give himself an erection and an orgasm.*

John:
You have never felt that I could have an orgasm. If you saw me, that would take away some of your doubt and that would help me.

A big step: John is to have an orgasm the way he usually does—adding only the presence of his wife.

Hilde:
I was lying on my side very close to him. He used strong pressure and the movements are very slow. He is very quiet. I felt good about being there. And very curious to see what would happen.

Suddenly, I saw that he had an orgasm. I expected him to have difficulty, but he came very easily. I was quite surprised.

John:

I was inhibited. I had some sort of performance stress, knowing that she expected a result. The orgasm—on a scale of one to ten—was a three. Clearly an orgasm, but too fast, too soon. It was the first time in five years I was not alone—and the orgasm was not as good.

Now John takes a second step away from his isolation: *he includes her touch.*

Hilde:

I am beginning to understand the pressure he needs. Saturday, we made love using my bare leg against his penis. I learned so much I had never known. It is the base of his penis that is the key to his arousal. Saturday, he had no orgasm, we had a lovely time without it. But Sunday morning, he was rested, very relaxed; I was more experienced. I pushed my leg against his penis. He rubbed back and forth and had a *forceful* ejaculation. I had never seen it. I was more than surprised. I was shocked.

Hilde is shocked that John has always been far more sexually functional than she thought. John gives up another one of his secrets. Another breakthrough. Now that he can have an orgasm in front of her, he can move closer to having an erection *with* her. But here's a catch: John and Hilde want John to have an erection, but they also want to do in bed what they've always done in bed. They are reluctant to give up "our way."

Giving Up the Best Orgasm

The third step: *John teaches Hilde to caress his penis with her hands. Hilde teaches John to caress her clitoris with his hands.* At this step, John balks. So does Hilde.

John:
    No, she doesn't know how. She doesn't know what I need.

True. He's never told her. She couldn't know. And he doesn't want her to know because then she'll know the secret he's kept from every woman: he has learned to *like* having an orgasm with 30 percent of an erection.

> I have found the perfect technique to get off. I squeeze my penis between my legs, giving the most pressure to the sensitive head of my penis . . . every day . . . I squeeze my penis back and forth until the feeling becomes so intense I ejaculate.
>
> When I do this, if I get a full erection my penis slips from between my legs. I lose the high feeling. There was a time after Gail left me when I still awoke with a full erection. I remember I would consciously think of nonsexual things to get my erection down so I could start working with my legs . . . that was the only way I got sexual relief. I suppose I could have kept the feeling if I used my hands on my penis, but I preferred to use only my legs—and that way *if I got an erection I would have no orgasm*—that 30 percent erection, that amount of softness, gave me the perfect orgasm. My splendid isolation . . . for many years in my life . . . has been so convenient. I didn't have to take the time *to go out with a woman*. I didn't have to spend money. I didn't have all the worry: "What will happen when we're alone?"

John has practiced his "splendid isolation" since he was a teenager. By the time he was with a woman there was nothing she could think of to do that could possibly give him the erotic high that he got with this highly developed touch of his legs against his penis. Of course, if he had told any woman exactly how to touch his penis to duplicate the exquisite feel he had developed with his legs, she could have done that, and right then he would have gotten an erection and had an orgasm. But John cannot tell a woman.

Without knowing her husband is reluctant to let her touch *his* genitals, Hilde says she's against his touching *her* genitals: "No. John can't do that."

Even though John is out of the room when she repeats the old secret, she whispers:

> My husband has an unnatural fear of my body below the waist. He can't touch me there. He would be very upset if I got excited and got even a tiny bit wet. Besides, I don't need his hands. I get what I want when I have his penis between my legs. I get my very best orgasm "our way."

The problem: John's soft penis gives both lovers their very best orgasm. What seems so simple—to take one more small step from their narrow path to a slightly broader path—is a major undertaking. Neither lover trusts the other's erotic use of hands. Besides, they know even if the lover does learn and either one of them does have an orgasm that way, it won't be as good as the orgasm they get from "our way." That's true. However, having the very best orgasm should not be their goal. Their goal should be to *add* erotic options to their sex life in small steps until they have such a wide number of erotic options and they are so erotically skillful that there will be no possibility of John's holding back his erections.

The third small step toward John's building his arousal high enough to get an erection is for each lover to learn to use his or her hands to bring the other lover to orgasm. The hands are the most erotic part of the body. And the *most underused* by impotent couples. Genital touch, his and hers, adds dramatic new options. After she learns how to caress his penis to orgasm with her hands, after he learns to caress her clitoris to orgasm with *his hands,* they will have new erotic choices.

The lovers distrust each other.

John:

> I am afraid she won't get it right. She never has. What she used to do in the past, touching my penis, felt pleasant—but not erotic. But then I never had the courage to tell her what "right" was.

Hilde:

> My husband can't touch my vagina. Just the breasts are interesting to him. For a year and a half I would take his hands and put

them between my legs. It seemed that he was interested and then I realized that he wasn't. He doesn't like to go into my body either with his hands or with his penis. It is uncomfortable for him. On two occasions he put his fingers into my vagina for less than a minute. I stopped it when I realized touching my vagina was a big effort for him. And I was right, he was so happy when everything was over. Now he's careful to go just to a certain point. He never stimulates my clitoris with his hands. He *can't do that.*

John tells Hilde a truth she finds hard to believe:

I was never *afraid* of your vagina. I never found any part of your body distasteful. I stayed away because once I touched you there I could not proceed. The computer in my head is going. I am always thinking, If I cannot get an erection, I should not be doing this. It is false advertising. I am thinking, Why should I go ahead if I cannot go ahead.

Hilde:

My impression is different.

John:

That is your assumption. Because I might feel reluctant—resistant even—I am not. I feel . . . I feel that when I touch you down there, it is like showing off. I feel like I am showing someone that I am ready to do more than I could actually perform.

Hilde:

I disagree. It is plain to see. We have done this for more than two years—*and* I have told you that I know you cannot do more. I accept that. And I do not expect more.

John:

I know that's what you *say,* but something deep inside me keeps me back. I know *you* don't expect me to, but I myself feel that if I touch you there, I feel I should be able to follow through and do normal, regular intercourse.

Given permission to stimulate his wife clitorally with his hands—to do only that without going any further to do anything with his penis—John hesitates.

John:
> I can excite her clitoris with my penis, but not with my hands. And, anyway, I don't think she will find my hands as exciting. She likes the closeness of the other way. She likes the imagination.

Hilde agrees:
> I do. I like "our way." He won't know how to do this. And I feel nervous. He will not like it if his hands get wet.

Impasse.
Which is exactly how they have kept themselves repeating the same kind of lovemaking for more than two years—the kind that fails to give John an erection. The two of them meet each other with reasons why they cannot possibly add to the sexual things they do.

- She won't get it right.
- He's afraid of my vagina.
- She wouldn't like it as well.
- I really tried to get him to change, but he won't.
- I can't do things that would lead him to ask me to do more.
- The orgasm wouldn't be as good.

To change from getting *no* erections to getting erections, the lovers have to do things differently. All the talk—all the reasons why they can't *do* the erotic acts necessary for the man to get erections is old news. Leap over it. *Do the next step.* After you give your lover the right touch, then talk.

John teaches Hilde how to touch his penis. He reports her success:

> She improved because I told her to start at the base of my penis. After I am at least half erect, I like to feel her hands squeezing—giving hard, slow pressure. With more erection, I want her to move to the head of the penis. To have an orgasm, even when I do it myself, I need stimulation of the tip of my penis.

As John teaches Hilde to be the best lover he could ever hope for, his anxiety goes down, his arousal goes up—*and*—triggers a 50 percent greater erection.

Hilde teaches John to touch her clitoris. She places his hand between her legs and tells him which touch increases her arousal and which touch decreases her arousal—what she likes more and what she likes less. Exact pressure. Exact movement. Exact speed. The lovers are surprised.

Hilde:

We tried this other way . . . by hand. [Lowers her voice.] And he was very good. In five minutes I had an orgasm. I was *very* surprised. He wasn't reluctant. All I said was: "A little bit faster. Not so strong." I also asked him to caress my breasts at the same time because this is very important to me.

John:

I am a good pupil. I learned that the touch should *not* be slow and with strong pressure. She likes faster with lighter pressure. I was surprised to learn how close I had been to perfection in the past. When she said, "Softer" if we were on a scale of one to ten, say she wanted three and I had been at five, I was within range. I expected to feel a bit foolish, but I did not feel like a complete beginner or a novice.

I could tell she was going to orgasm by her way of breathing faster, getting excited, but I had no sense of this by my hands on her clitoris.

I felt a nice, pleasant feeling that I could do something for Hilde. I was eager to do it. It was rewarding, for me, to be able to give something to her.

I feel more relaxed, less mechanical. I got more pleasure this time. I feel more involved because I know this is the first step. I am encouraged by having a direction. Now I have hope. And I feel warmer.

John sees new possibilities—new hope—for several reasons. The man who can bring his lover to orgasm with his hands is less dependent on always having to have an erection. Less pressure. Up goes the arousal.

The man who allows his lover to teach him what she wants is certain to be a successful lover. Less pressure. Up goes the arousal.

John:
  Our relationship is becoming closer. That is a surprise.

Hilde:
  I feel so odd because I was convinced we *were* very close.

The surprise is the new closeness. They thought they had been close, but John—as well as Hilde—had been shut out. Isolated. As they become more erotically involved, their love deepens. They smile at each other. They look eagerly into each other's eyes. John holds Hilde's hand. Hilde puts her arms around his waist.

They are ready for the fourth small step: John is to move from having a partial erection to having a full erection.

Breaking the Partial-Erection Habit

The danger is the orgasm. Having an orgasm is a very enjoyable experience. It's a reward. So whatever occurs immediately *before* orgasm—John's 30 percent erection—tends to occur more and more often—until his rewarded 30 percent erection becomes his standard erection.

A common problem. Many men get themselves stuck in the partial-erection pattern. One man has had surgery and because his body hurts, he ejaculates a few times with only a partial erection. Later the discomfort is gone, but the partial erection pattern remains. Another man—underaroused—comes with a partial erection, comes again—and the partial-erection pattern remains.

To break the partial-erection pattern, change the reward system. Never have an orgasm unless your erection is slightly greater than it was the last time. John has to give up his pattern of the "best" orgasm at 30 percent erection. Hilde is to look at his penis to judge the size of his erection and to hold him back—the next orgasm is allowed *only* after he reaches 40 percent erection. And the next only after he reaches 50 percent. And so on, until he is regularly having orgasms at 100 percent. And if he doesn't meet the criteria? There is no orgasm.

The new orgasms will not feel as erotic *at first*. That's how he got stuck in this pattern in the first place: sticking with the erotic feeling of a partial-erection orgasm. The way out is to choose the larger erection *over* the best orgasm. Temporarily. Your body is *very* adaptable erotically. Which is—again—the way John adapted so well to having orgasms with a partial erection. The body that adapts to having an orgasm with a partial erection will also adapt to having an orgasm with a full erection— *after* the new pattern is established.

Breaking the partial-erection pattern requires that Hilde build his arousal slightly higher each time they make love. She is able to do that because he now trusts her with a great deal of formerly secret information.

John:

I wish for particular procedures. I like a shower with my lover, then to be dried and relaxed, lying on the bed. I like that feeling of being close to you. I want you to touch my scrotum lightly, very lightly, scrotum and the upper inside of my legs. With a lotion is better—light slippery touch relaxes me completely. Scrotal touch prepares me for arousal.

I want both your hands around the base of my penis holding *strong*—a strong grip. Much stronger than you could stand on your genitals.

Hilde:

Using my hands in just the way he said, I gave him his biggest erection, 60 percent, maybe 70 percent. He lost it when he got in position with his penis against my leg. The leg-to-penis step we had been using was less effective. I used my hand to hold his penis against my thigh—and his penis became erect again.

In past months without the understanding between them that they could do things to build his arousal, she would have accepted the 30 percent erection. The pattern would have held. Now at each point the pattern is broken.

Each time they make love, they switch roles: He caresses her to orgasm *or* she caresses him to orgasm. When she caresses him she takes the responsibility for recognizing the larger erection. She moves slowly, following his directions and using her hands more expertly, so that each time she touches him his erection increases slightly. He prefers a strong grip at the base of his penis, she gives him that. He prefers a certain touch at the tip of his penis, she gives him that. His arousal shoots up. His erection increases.

The lovers have barely noticed a significant change—John has an erection—with his wife—most of the time. Hilde says with a trace of disbelief: "He can penetrate just because he wants to."

Eight weeks after John first explored the erotic sensitivity of Hilde's arms and hands they have what they call a "small miracle." John is erect. Hilde grasps the base of his penis, she puts his penis in her vagina, he thrusts as he stimulates her clitoris. She, after two or three minutes, orgasms—and her "hopelessly impotent" lover is still erect!

The Dangers of Having "Normal" Sex (Reprise)

The week that John reports he feels that his erections are established, Hilde changes.

Hilde, the "I always have an orgasm" woman, the "I have no sex problems" lover, shows she also has her limits. Having taught John how to touch her clitoris, she sinks back into her comfortable silence. Soon John is once again off the mark. She once again prefers he stop trying.

> His hands are too rough. Too many bones. I prefer his soft penis.

Hilde is talking about pressure. It is *not* the soft penis *v.* the bony hands, it is simply soft *v.* rough. She *prefers* light pressure on her clitoris. Taught never to talk about sex, she wants to feel a man touching her clitoris lightly and slowly *without* telling him she wants it. And absolutely without having to tell him over and over.

Asked if her lover, when he was so good with his hands, was as good as she would be with her own hands, Hilde makes a startling confession:

> I could never masturbate myself—even in private—because it doesn't work. You are a braver man than I could be. I could never touch my clitoris. I never could. Never.

At the suggestion that John put Hilde's hand on his and teach her how to touch her own clitoris—so they can add yet another option to their repertoire—she recoils, raises her voice emphatically, and says: *"No, I don't like it!"* Another secret exposed: It is Hilde who has a "morbid fear of her vagina" and of her own natural lubrication. It is Hilde who would be upset to feel herself if she "should get even a little bit wet."

Impasse.

Sweet, understanding Hilde, who imagines she never pressures her husband, pressures him by being reluctant to let him touch her clitoris and by refusing to touch her clitoris herself. His limp penis gives her the soft pressure she loves, without her having to say one word, and certainly without her having to touch herself. So does his erection thrusting in her vagina until she comes. Either one of these will do. That's what she wants. And, as Hilde says repeatedly, "I get what I want."

When it is suggested that while they may enjoy penis-in-the-vagina intercourse, it may not be their favorite activity or their only activity but may simply take its place as one of the many options in the sexual repertoire, Hilde declares her wish to always have sex "the normal way."

Forgetting entirely about the many erotic options she and her lover have developed over the last three months, Hilde is adamant:

> I am thirty-five. John is not my first man. With other men I have always liked to have intercourse and I will like it with my husband.

Hilde is in danger of making penis-in-the-vagina intercourse her "narrow path." Hilde has planned to take responsibility until John gets his erection back and then fall into her old pattern of once again making sex his responsibility. They both plan to take up a life of sex by the numbers. One, he hugs her and kisses her. Two, he caresses her breasts. Three, he penetrates and thrusts. She comes. He comes.

Wrong plan.

Too few numbers. Now that, as John says, they can "do it the right way," they make the disastrous decision to limit their eroticism to four sequential acts—with John once again in charge of each move. Being so quick to abandon the many erotic ways of touching that they have so painstakingly learned shows that John and Hilde are still confused about what was wrong with their sex life to begin with. It wasn't that John's masturbation was wrong or that having a super orgasm through soft touch of a lover's penis was wrong; what went wrong is that those activities became carved in stone. The lovers could do nothing else. Now they can be erotic every which way, and they plan to let that wonderful possibility go—in favor of having sex "the normal way."

That plan leads directly back to impotence. The lovers are re-creating John's original circumstance—the circumstance in which John felt too much pressure to get an erection and too little erotic touch to maintain an erection after he got one. To maintain his erections John needs what every man needs: a lover who shares the responsibility, one with whom he can enjoy a thousand pleasures. And one with whom he can be his natural, biological male self—a creature whose erections come and go. Unfortunately, John finds it nearly impossible to follow step 4: learn to feel comfortable losing your erection in front of a woman.

Learning to Lose Your Erection in Front of Her

This is supposed to be a great disgrace. We have been taught to believe the man must keep his erection throughout lovemaking by people who have innocently passed on an erotic tradition based on secrets and lies and primitive beliefs.

John has gone beyond his cultural tradition. On those few occasions when his body is too tired or too anxious or too anything to give him an erection, he can still make love. He has options: He can touch her clitoris till she orgasms; he can have oral sex; she can touch his genitals till he orgasms—his penis against her thigh, his penis in her hands, his penis in her hands with lotion, her hands building his arousal by grasping the base of his penis.

With all his new skills, all his new erotic options, all the new confidence that he's built, step by step, with Hilde, John—like many men—has one vestigial worry: What if I lose my erection?

What will happen? Nothing much. His penis is still there. The lovers fear that, once lost, the erection is gone forever. False. It is always okay for John to lose his erection because he knows how to touch his penis to raise his arousal and he has taught Hilde exactly how to do the same.

Therefore, any time either of them touches his penis in that exact way, his arousal will go up and he will get an erection.

If both lovers feel comfortable about letting John follow his natural biology—getting an erection, losing an erection, getting an erection—they can help each other learn how to kill John's anxiety at the very second it starts, which is the most crucial skill for any lovers who want to rid themselves forever of erection problems. To do that follow step 5: stop trying harder.

How to Stop Trying Harder

John has to learn to recognize the pattern that makes him want to try to keep his erection. And then he has to disrupt the pattern. Unfortunately, John and Hilde rather quickly establish the traditional pattern of too many couples: a kiss and a hug, breast caress, penetration, thrusting and orgasm. Over and over and over. They are used to going from start to finish always the same. They fear disruption—yet the *pattern* puts extreme pressure on John.

Hilde:

>Two times, maybe three, he has had a 70 percent erection. He entered me about two inches. He had every ability to penetrate deeper. I have the impression my husband could have done more. He had the approval to go deeper into my vagina, but he stopped. He lost his erection. He is afraid.

Her expectations. His expectations. He's back to the initial point that got his body into this trouble in the first place. Once again, he tries too hard.

John:

>When I penetrate I feel a little bit nervous. I worry about . . . getting soft . . . falling out. I associate penetration with having to keep my erection as long as it takes to finish the job. After penetration it's all serious business. There's no playing around. That makes me think: Am I sufficiently erect? Will I be able to maintain my erection?

Wrong thinking. There is *always* playing around. Lovemaking is *not* business. Or football. You can always stop. There is never a time when you have to keep running with that one erection to make the orgasm. And if there is such a time—when your lover pressures you to try harder or you pressure you to try harder—stop. At each point where you expect to *have* to get an erection or keep an erection—break the expectancy.

How?

Change what you do with your lover so there is no one event that pressures you to keep an erection. When John feels the least bit of anxiety, he is to stop and switch to a different erotic touch. When Hilde notices that John is becoming anxious, she is to disrupt the pattern.

Every time he feels worried that he might lose his erection—before he thinks—he tries harder to keep his erection.

Wrong action.

Tightening or pushing or tensing up stops blood flow. Do the opposite. Stop trying at all. Back off. Relax. Nearly impossible for John. A man who built his exceptional business career on "trying harder" has a hard time handling a problem by trying less. Trying harder is John's instinctive reaction to all of life's problems. However, making love is different from anything else we do.

Luckily, when making love, a man has a lover. Hilde can recognize when John is tightening up before he realizes it. Hilde can feel John try harder. She is to say, "Stop." They are to play erotically until his penis stiffens again naturally—or they are to play erotically with no intention of using his stiff penis.

Penetration is the event that pressures John.

Solution: Hilde takes charge of a variety of penetration sex *play*. Once Hilde understands that John was reluctant to penetrate deeper because he felt pressured by the event itself, and once she knows there is something she can do that will change that for John, she is eager to do it. She teaches John to play erotically with penetration rather than "working to finish the job." Hilde puts his erect penis in her vagina. She strokes the base of his penis, then she raises herself—and caresses his thighs. Another time she caresses his penis against the outside of her vagina until he ejaculates. One time she has an orgasm while he thrusts, another time she raises herself and puts his hand on her clitoris to bring her to orgasm that way. Hilde smiles and says this is one of the most fun games she has ever played.

The *event* that signals a man to try harder could be anything. He could feel pressured to get an erection and keep an erection whenever his lover takes her clothes off. He could feel pressured every time he gets in bed with a lover. Whatever the event, the solution is the same: Stop. Do nothing. Break the pattern.

On his own, the man who instinctually pushes to get ahead in every situation may be unaware that he ever tries too hard, and therefore be unable to use the solution, but his lover can notice his tension and destroy it. She can say: Stop. Do nothing. She can break the pattern. And she should be encouraged to do so.

The event may come well before penetration. Special ways of preparing the bedroom, putting on a condom, and fear of losing an erection are common causes of trying too hard and share a similar solution.

- *Lighting candles.* When his wife lights the candles near their bed, he knows she wants to have intercourse, so he tenses his body to try to get an erection.

Solution: She lights the candles—and then proceeds to do everything—forbidding him to use his erection.

Another time he and she have intercourse in the dark. Another time they have intercourse in the afternoon. Another time she lights candles and they just talk.

- *Putting on a condom.* When he goes to get the condom, he worries excessively about keeping his erection through this "break in the action."

Solution: let your lover be in charge of a *variety of sex play* with the condoms. Same night. Many different erotic touches. She puts the condom on his erect penis, she strokes the base of his penis, she takes the condom off. Later, she puts another condom on, puts his penis in her vagina, he withdraws, she takes the condom off, strokes his penis till he comes. After that, they are playing around, she puts a condom on his erect penis, they do nothing but play around. They play around like this until there are condoms all over the bed.

- *Fear of losing the erection.* He tries harder every time he feels he might lose his erection. The moment he switches his concentration to trying *directly* to keep the blood trapped in his penis, the blood eases away and his penis falls out of her vagina.

Solution: When she feels him trying harder, she says, "Stop trying harder." They switch to erotic touches that do not require an erection.

How long do you need to switch patterns? As long as he feels penetration means he must continue to orgasm. As long as he feels anxious. Less anxiety means less practice. And what if the anxiety should return? Then repeat. Once again disrupt the "I must orgasm" cycle.

Recognition of the first seconds of anxiety that come with trying harder may be the single most important skill of successful lovers.

At the point John and Hilde have the skill to keep John from going wrong they can keep him getting strong healthy erections. Always.

The Skill of the Lover Assured of Success

John changes. The man who always suggested sex to his wife in the most gentlemanly ways and took back the offer at the slightest sign of her hesitancy, becomes sexually aggressive. John wants sex.

She shuffled into the bedroom carrying a tray with our breakfast coffee. She was rumpled, barely awake, in her black nightgown. In the morning I am instantly awake. I looked at her nipples pushing the silky material and I didn't think about anything. I grabbed her, pulled her on top of me, penetrated—and, in less than a minute I came. I thought about sex at work . . . having sex with her. I was exhausted after work but I still wanted her. I licked her clitoris. I tickled her there. Licked her nipples. Sucked. Penetrated. She had her orgasm in record time. I had my orgasm as we used to—against her leg. That was Monday. On Thursday—I can't remember—she had an orgasm and then I did a few seconds later. Friday night we had such a pleasant experience. We went back to "our way." Hilde had a magnificent orgasm. We went to sleep—and then about three

A.M. I woke her. I began to move my penis along her leg, back and forth. She grasped the base of my penis, caressed the whole length, varying the touch in the way I taught her, I put my full weight on her body, penetrated, thrust, I stopped, I played with her clitoris with my erect penis still inside her. She wanted more, she grasped hard with her vagina, she was moaning and moaning ... and I can't remember. That was the best. One of the best.

And what happens on those few occasions when John loses his erection? Sometimes she mouths the sensitive head of his penis, and naturally he gets an erection. Sometimes he licks her bellybutton, and naturally he gets an erection. Sometimes she touches the sensitive inner part of his thighs in the way he likes best, and naturally he gets an erection. Sometimes he tenderly fingers her nipples and naturally he gets an erection. Sometimes she does nothing. Sometimes he does nothing. And naturally he gets an erection. And another one. And another one. And another one.

HER ORGASM
How to Let Your Lover Help You, Why You May Not Want To, and Why You Should Anyway

George wanted to do it, so we did. I always wait till George wants to. Last night, he barely kissed me. He played with my breasts and I loved it. He pinched. He licked, he sucked. He sucked on the edge of the nipple, then took the whole nipple in his mouth and sucked very hard. I am wild about that. But it went by so fast.

George wants to "get right to it," so I tried, but it ... I knew it wouldn't work. Getting right to it never works.

Let's see, he put my hand on his penis. I never know what I'm supposed to do then, so I slid my fingers up and down a couple of times and stopped. He climbed on top, put his dick in—that was a struggle. I am dry down there. He caught the lips of my vagina and pushed them in with his penis. It hurt, I used to tell him it hurt ... well, I told him once, but he didn't seem to notice. He came pretty fast. Well, I always want him to come fast because I'm dry and screwing hurts.

I worry, well, you know, that I'm not very good in bed. I feel . . . so little. I love George. But, in bed, nothing much. No orgasm. I never even feel like I might be getting close.

Sex Without Trust

Making love in a way that prevents a woman from having an orgasm is an unnatural act. Dorothy is supposed to feel erotically delighted. Her body is biologically geared toward orgasm. She—like all women—is supposed to have an orgasm. It's a matter of doing the right things in the right order to build his arousal so high that, beyond her control, her body lets go in orgasmic ecstasy. The problem: she stops herself. And so does George.

Trust is the issue.

> Dorothy needs to trust George.
> George needs to trust Dorothy.
> And they both need to trust Dorothy's body.

Failure to lubricate or have an orgasm is caused by one thing: insufficient arousal. More than 85 percent of healthy women—once they learn to raise their arousal—will have orgasms. Dorothy, once she knows the secrets, can easily have an orgasm any time she desires.

However, without the sex therapist's special knowledge of how easy Dorothy's success might be, she and George are harboring unhappy thoughts.

Dorothy:

I distrust men. Some bad things happened to me when I was little, with . . . well, you know . . . I had a cousin . . . older . . . well, the thing is . . . men are selfish. Men don't really care about women. Well, you know, they don't know what a woman needs. I don't know. Seems as though it's useless. Unless a man does everything just right, I don't feel anything; and they never do. Sometimes I feel . . . well, that I'll never have an orgasm.

His mother and my mother ... that's another pressure. They were friends when we were babies. Mother has a picture of George hugging me with his little baby-fat cheek against mine when I was two. So mom is always asking me how things are going ... and I always say fine and she always says, "George is a real sweet boy, isn't he," and I always say, "He is, he's real sweet."

How was I to know he was going to be a lousy lover ... I mean guys don't wear signs around their necks or anything.

I saw him for the first time. This is embarrassing. Really, I wanted to go to bed with him the second I saw him. He was playing baseball in the city park, municipal league ball, I think they call it. He put his jacket around my shoulders ... I don't know ... I ... I ... I ... couldn't get near enough to him. ... I had, you might say, a skin fetish. I wanted to be near his skin. I wanted to wash his back, to sleep in his shirt. I wanted to climb all over George. I wanted him under me, over me, on me—in me. I wanted him every way there was.

I was sure this was love at first sight, the perfect love, especially when he turned out to be so nice to me. George does everything for me. But I can't deal with sex with him. And now I have doubts ... about ... about, I don't even know if there is love ... or what.

My mother was repressed. She acted as though sex didn't even exist, so my grandmother told me about sex, and it's like what she said. There's nothing to know. If you're really in love, what a man and a woman do together is beautiful. Now I feel like I still have to find the man who I really love, another man who is right for me ... with him sex is going to be so easy.

This ... with George ... I feel ... well, degraded ... sort of. Anyway we got together so fast ... it's ... Maybe this is the first indication that all we have is infatuation masquerading as love.

By the end of her explanation, Dorothy is crying. "What do you do," she asks, "when you love someone but the sex is no good?"

George:

She puzzles me. She is ... what can I say ... she is sensitive to me. She knows what I'm feeling. I've told Dorothy stuff nobody else knows. I love her for that. And her laugh. And I swear I just

129

like the way she breathes. There's a lady ... honest to God ... I'd put my arm in the fire for her.

I was telling my mom I might get married, and she was real happy. And then she started me thinking. She was telling me how marriage was forever, really forever. So I am thinking about Dorothy lying there like a board every time I want to screw her, and being that way forever. I didn't like thinking about that.

That's really weird, how women have so much trouble coming. I don't think she likes sex. She's a schoolteacher, with eight-year-olds all the time. Maybe that has something to do with it. A couple of times I was really working on her. I was pumping away for hours. Well, it seemed like hours and I don't think she even hit first base. I guess that means she's frigid.

Interesting theory, but there is no such condition. Frigid is an obsolete term. Twenty years ago people believed that failing to have an orgasm and failing to love were the same thing: they called that frigidity. However, being able to build your arousal so high you have an orgasm, and loving someone, are two totally separate things. A cold woman can be so erotically skillful she has orgasms in seconds, while a loving woman can be so shy about erotic touch that she fails to have an orgasm ever.

Dorothy is naturally warm and loving. The battle: he says she's frigid, and she says it's his fault.

Dorothy:
How could I know he was going to be so ... stupid about women. Now how am I supposed to tell him ... I can't, I wouldn't hurt him like that ... I still love him.

Well, I sort of let him know once that he wasn't the greatest lover ... indirectly ... I said, "Does it ever hurt you when you make love?" He didn't pick up on it at all. He said no and gave me this weird look. Well, that is when we first started going together. I didn't care. ... Just being near George was ... that's all I wanted. Anyway, it's easier to just please George.

But, actually, "just pleasing George" is an illusion. George, in fact, is not at all pleased.

I love Dorothy. Sex now . . . well, sex is something else. Dorothy changes. Well, at first, she used to giggle and play around a little. Now she . . . she lies there doing nothing, like she's doing her duty or something.

George is right; when they make love, Dorothy changes. The moment he touches her, Dorothy wraps herself in an invisible cloak. She says nothing, she feels nothing. Dorothy waits.

In her mind she is *doing something*. She imagines that by tolerating everything George does—by just lying there—she is protecting their relationship, but doing nothing is no protection. What she fails to take into account is George's desire. So much of every man's desire—including George's—depends on his ability to make her wildly erotically happy. When he fails, he feels let down.

It just seems like she can't relax and let go. She holds herself in. I don't know what to do, but I know it would just make it worse if I said anything. Dorothy is the type of really good woman with whom you have to move slowly with sex. What I've been hoping, you know . . . I don't want to do anything to offend her . . . because, well, I'm going to ask her to marry me . . . and, well, marriage might do it. I'm hoping when she understands that this is forever and that I'm the one she can really relax with, she'll get loose and . . . be . . . I bet she could be really sexy.

That is George's first idea. But as the days go by, something keeps him from asking her, and while George keeps his marriage plans a secret, Dorothy develops a big secret of her own: she plans to leave him.

George says I can feel what he feels. His brother died. Cancer. And before he even told me I could feel his sadness. I wanted to take care of him. And I liked . . . well, I'd come home and he would have been there and left me flowers. . . . This girlfriend of mine, Marcia, she's . . . well, she doesn't even know what a sex problem is . . . everything about sex has always been easy for Marcia. I told her I was having some trouble with sex with him—no details. "Well," she said, "what can you expect, he's a dumb jock." But he's not dumb—well, George is not super sophisticated. . . . He's, well, what my grandmother would call the salt of the earth. George is the kind of man that is so hard to find in these days of easy sex—a thoroughly kind, compassionate human being.

Sex is just too important to give up. It's . . . I've got a long life ahead of me . . . I don't want to be an old lady alone with my cats. I have to give myself a chance to find a guy who is good in bed.

Through Dorothy's talk runs a decisive theme: *My sex life has nearly nothing to do with me.* And she is most definite in her idea about woman's orgasm. Woman's orgasm, she believes, is up to the man.

My fantasy of the perfect sex life is . . . well, it's kind of embarrassing . . . and I wouldn't want you to get it wrong. It's from that silly movie, *American Gigolo,* about a male prostitute. But my fantasy has nothing to do with the guy who played the prostitute or the movie—it was only this one part. The guy is bragging about how he gave this woman an orgasm. She was an older woman, a widow, who hadn't had an orgasm for fifteen years. He made love to her for three hours. *Three hours.* And, after trying everything, when he had nearly given up hope, she came. At the end of his story, he looks into the camera with this real sincere expression and says, "Who else would take the time?" That's what I see as the perfect relationship, a man who will take the time, no matter how long, to learn what arouses me . . . a man totally interested in knowing what I am about sexually . . . and emotionally.

Dorothy is waiting. Waiting for the man who will give her an orgasm. Wrong plan.

A man who will do everything to her body forever, that's what Dorothy sees as the perfect relationship. But actually the lovers in her fantasy, instead of having the perfect relationship, have, in fact, almost no relationship—though, as with all fantasy lovers, they do have sensually blissfully, erotic, ecstatic sex anyway.

Inherent in this fantasy is the idea that there is some universal woman's body and that some men really know what women like—and some men don't.

That, of course, is a wrong idea. Every woman's body—and every man's body—is unique. What if George did touch Dorothy's unique body every erotic way for three hours? Dorothy would still be afraid to tell him what she feels inside her body. She keeps her erotic wishes a deep, dark secret. Secret, of course, from George—but what George doesn't know is that Dorothy has kept the same secret from every lover she's ever had, and unfortunately even from herself.

Rather than trying to discover her secrets, George looks for the purely medical remedy. But that won't work. Biologically, Dorothy is perfect. When she kisses George her nipples erect. During thrusting her clitoris enlarges and withdraws under its hood. Blood rushes into the walls of her vagina about every ninety minutes while she sleeps. All her involuntary arousal systems work perfectly.

But George is sure they don't. He's sure Dorothy has a biological problem, and he has proof.

> She told me she didn't think her vagina was very sensitive. I was sympathetic. I told her I suspected something like that. I told her that most women have very sensitive vaginas. She just kept on about it, saying she wasn't so sure she could feel much there. She said even when she jammed her vagina with a Tampax holder she didn't feel much. That was scary to hear. And I did feel bad for her. I figured maybe there was something wrong with her vagina. I read about a woman with her problem in *The Godfather*—a real young woman who didn't feel anything in her vagina so she went to this surgeon who tightened it up for her. And then she was fine. I told her she really ought to go see a doctor.

So, while Dorothy is dreaming of three hours of perfect erotic touch at the hands of a Hollywood fantasy and George is planning for Dorothy to have unnecessary surgery, neither one realizes how little they really have to do to enjoy each other erotically.

Facts About Lubricating and Having an Orgasm

Women get erections. Although what happens in their bodies isn't exactly the same as what happens in a man's body, women do go through an extraordinarily similar biological process. Women have similar blood flow. The same arousal system. Same variability. The same erotic arousal triggers the autonomic nervous system to send Dorothy's blood rushing into two areas in the walls of her vagina. Her vagina tightens and gets hard. The blood pushing against her mucous membrane causes her to lubricate. The blood engorging the two spaces in the outer third of her vagina is of equal volume to the blood holding his penis erect. In both cases, getting the blood there depends on building arousal.

Blood flow causes lubrication. It's a nearly simultaneous response. In the heat of passion, her blood rushes into the walls of her vagina, where it stays trapped. Lubrication.

Because they don't know one of the basic secrets of sex therapy, Dorothy and George worry over a part of Dorothy's biology that happens naturally without her doing anything.

No need to worry.

Lubricating the Natural Way

Any time Dorothy wants to lubricate, all she has to do is go to sleep. Every ninety minutes during her periods of rapid-eye-movement sleep, her blood rushes into her vaginal walls causing her to lubricate. The biology of vaginal lubrication is automatic; not only automatic, but ready to be activated with the slightest help. Dorothy and George conspire to stop it.

He played with my breasts and I loved it.

That erotic sensation sends Dorothy's autonomic nervous system into action. She begins to lubricate.

But it went by so fast.

George stops. At that moment her arousal drops. What happens in her body is similar to a man's losing an erection. The blood eases out of her vaginal walls; she stops lubricating.

He . . . put his dick in—that was a struggle. I am dry down there. . . . It hurt.

Feeling his penis in her vagina raises her arousal slightly. It's a mixed message. She also feels the unpleasant sensations—the irritation of his dry penis against her dry vagina; that lowers her arousal.

The importance of doing things in the right order. Dorothy's erotic biology is remarkably similar to George's. The same degree of arousal produces the same reflexes and in the same order. First the erection and then the orgasm.

The woman's vaginal wall is *supposed* to fill with blood and the wall is supposed to lubricate. That reflex is supposed to occur *before* penetration. When Dorothy and George rush forward to penetration before Dorothy's body is ready, they've started a struggle against nature.

There is an often-told lie that a woman—unlike a man—can always have sex. But it is reproductive sex that she can always have. For erotic sex, she needs to build her arousal high enough so her blood flows into her vaginal walls and her vaginal mucous membrane gets slippery. Without those biological changes she has little genital sensitivity. She is impotent.

She can't see exactly what's happening, so she is shielded from the preoccupation with the exact size of her blood congestion. Being unable to see the size of her vaginal hardening, she is unlikely to suffer from the erection anxiety men get when they overreact to temporary erection loss.

That's the good news. The bad news is that because her erection is hidden, her lovers often act as though it isn't there.

While George would never dream of penetrating or trying to have an orgasm *before* he got an erection, he quite innocently rushes Dorothy past that step, and then they both expect that some way or other she will magically get very excited and come. But with so little arousal, her blood barely moves into her vaginal walls; and with so little blood there, she can't possibly lubricate. Then, without that erotic base, she can't possibly build her arousal high enough to have an orgasm. About five minutes after he and Dorothy are naked, George makes his first mistake: he penetrates and thrusts *before* she lubricates. And it's then that Dorothy makes hers: she lets him. Naturally, at that point her body does what it must— her body blocks erotic sensation. As it is with men, Dorothy's problem has nothing to do with fit; her problem is one of arousal. And blood flow. Her vagina tightens by itself if she gets excited enough.

Which brings us back to trust. All Dorothy has to do to have one marvelously sensual experience after another with George is to tell him how to touch her to build her arousal to lubrication, and then tell him more about how to build her arousal high enough to orgasm.

How do the lovers build Dorothy's arousal high enough? The same way everyone does. Touching, feeling touched, feeling passion, doing things in order. First, establish an arousal level that keeps the blood in the walls of the vagina or the penis, and, only after that, build the arousal higher, higher, higher so the heart beats faster, the body heats higher, the lovers breathe faster, the clitoris withdraws, nearly disappearing under its hood. Dorothy passes the point of no return.

Beyond her control, the muscles surrounding the outer third of her vagina contract rhythmically every .8 second. Unseen, her cervix widens, her uterus rises and contracts. Orgasm.

Orgasms: Easy, Better, Best

Mounds of pages have been written on how to get the easy orgasm, the better orgasm, the best orgasm.

Which orgasm is easy? For most people, it's the orgasm they give themselves by touching their genitals the way they like. The easiest orgasm is the one George gives himself by touching his penis. Right? Right. The easiest orgasm is the one Dorothy can give herself by touching her vagina. Right? Not necessarily.

Dorothy can orgasm more easily by touching her clitoris.

Which orgasm is better? Nearly everyone reports the same thing: The orgasm I have with my lover is *better*. The orgasm with a lover, however, is often more difficult because of the great difference between the sexes. The most highly sensitive part of the man's body is his penis; for the woman it is her clitoris. The problem: during penis-in-the-vagina intercourse, the clitoris may be untouched.

And there's where Dorothy and George make their second mistake. George believes that since he receives such enormous pleasure from having his penis inside his lover's vagina, she must be feeling the identical sensations; often the woman assumes she should, too; sometimes she assumes she is. He makes this mistake because he uses *his* genitals as a guide to *her* genitals. He gets his greatest erotic high from stimulation of his penis, so he assumes that Dorothy's vagina, being the equivalent of the penis, must be where she feels the most sensitively erotic.

Wrong assumption.

The vagina is *not* the female equivalent of the penis. The vagina is far less sensitive. It has to be, because the vagina is the birth canal. The *clitoris* is the female equivalent of the penis. The clitoris is exquisitely sensitive. So is the penis. For Dorothy—like most women—trying to have an orgasm without anything touching her clitoris would be like George (or most men) trying to have an orgasm without anything touching his penis—it's *possible*, but decidedly more difficult.

Men exploring to find out exactly where their lover's vagina is most sensitive have found dead spots where the woman is completely insensitive for no apparent reason; they have also found dead spots surrounding old giving-birth scars; and they have also found sensitive areas. Sometimes by simply changing positions so his penis thrusts against a more sensitive area the woman finds a wonderful new erotic high. Which position? There is no one position that's best for all women. Every woman is different. There is no universal vagina. There is no mechanical way to approach a lover's vagina, no spot to push. There is only finding out what is true for each woman's one-and-only body.

The vagina—though less sensitive than the clitoris—*is* sensitive. Researchers have found the outer third, near the opening—the part that fills with blood—to be the most sensitive. Muscles surrounding the vagina do contract every .8 second in orgasm. The question: where is the path to the orgasm?

Nearly 70 percent of women report they must have clitoral stimulation to have an orgasm. If 70 percent of men—as might be the case—reported they had to have penile stimulation to orgasm, none of us would bat an eyelash. However, a woman's experiences with clitoral excitement may confuse her. Because the clitoris and vagina are very near each other, the erotic sensations blend. If George would caress Dorothy's clitoris, her clitoris would enlarge and harden and feel highly erotic *and* that caress would trigger a rush of blood to her vagina which would lubricate. For a woman and a man to have the best orgasm and the easiest, together, they have to find a way to stimulate the penis *and the clitoris*.

Short thrusts v. long? Sometimes when George penetrates deep into Dorothy's vagina and moves in and out a *short* distance, his abdomen may come repeatedly up against her clitoral area and this could increase her arousal until she orgasms. However, many men find this gives their penis too little stimulation to get *their* arousal high enough for orgasm. Like most men, George gets his greatest arousal from thrusting in *long* strokes. A few women do, too. This thrusting pulls the clitoral skin in and down over the clitoral hood, and for a very few women this is sufficient to produce orgasm. Or Dorothy might assume a position such as woman on top, which places her clitoris where it can be continually stimulated by his pubis. With any of these techniques she might achieve an orgasm which would *appear* to happen solely by vaginal stimulation.

Unable to give up the idea that reproductive sex and erotic sex *are* the same thing, the traditional male has sometimes been known to cling desperately to the "her vagina is just like my penis" theory. It makes lovemaking so much easier for him. An Ohio doctor has gone so far as to design an operation to correct nature's deficiency. For a fee, he will move Dorothy's clitoris inside her vagina. He reports having many satisfied couples. Another doctor claims he has found a spot—the spot in every woman's vagina—which *is* just like his penis. Rub that spot, have an orgasm. And there are still many people who, in the face of God's divine plan for the female body, will say, "No. God was wrong. Having the most erotic organ outside of the vagina is a mistake." Or, "No. I don't believe scientific reports. I believe the vagina is the most sensitive female organ."

The debate is endless. And worthless.

So?

How does this help Dorothy?

Or George?

So 70 percent of American women say they need direct clitoral stimulation to orgasm. So two women in Ohio get direct clitoral stimulation inside their vaginas. So one woman in Omaha, Nebraska, swears she has a vaginal orgasm—totally vaginal. Dorothy and George still have to discover how they, with their unique bodies, can have the most exquisite pleasure together. The answer is not in a book or in claims of people they don't know. They have the answer. It's there in Dorothy's body. It's a unique secret between each woman and her lover.

Which is the best orgasm? Clitoral stimulation to orgasm was considered by Freud to be infantile. The best woman's orgasm was vaginal. Because of new evidence that thrusting produces the *secondary stimulation of the clitoris,* later experts have expressed doubt about whether a pure vaginal orgasm exists. Should Dorothy care?

Research shows that there is *little difference between orgasms produced by different types of sexual stimulation.*

Dorothy's friend Marcia objects:

No, that cannot be true. Really, I have a wonderful orgasm during cunnilingus, but have a weak orgasm during masturbation. I have never had a vaginal orgasm, but, really, I want to—just to find out if that's even better.

Again, according to the research: there is little difference between orgasms produced by different types of sexual stimulation.

Still, Marcia is right. *If* her erotic preference is cunnilingus, cunnilingus will give her the ultimate orgasm. However, if your erotic preference is making love underwater, with three short thrusts, five long thrusts, knees tied together with silk ribbons, tongue down your lover's throat, that will give you your ultimate orgasm.

Each person's eroticism is uniquely theirs. Though George and Dorothy can help themselves immeasurably by understanding the basic facts of their erotic biology, perhaps the most important fact to understand is that the ultimate orgasm cannot be dictated by biology.

The issue is not whether the vaginal orgasm, clitoral orgasm, masturbatory orgasm, or anal orgasm is best. The answer isn't even in the body; the answer is in the mind. Once Dorothy gets the eroticism she loves, she will love the orgasm that follows. Your way of having an orgasm—if you really like your way—is as good as anybody else's way.

The danger occurs when someone tells you it is a *natural law* that long thrusts with ice against the testicles always produce the ultimate orgasms for everybody. People sometimes believe their body gives them the ultimate orgasm, but no one's body does. It is the love, the passion, the erotic ideas we bring to what we do with our bodies that give each of us our greatest orgasm. So it makes no difference what any person says is the best orgasm, it is right: each person does enjoy best what he or she has learned to enjoy best.

Multiple orgasms and longer-lasting orgasms. An orgasm is that reflex action that hinges on your genital muscles contracting every .8 second. Physiologically every contraction is nearly like the last. Some are a few seconds longer. Some women have them in a series. How do they do that? There is no training procedure to follow to get yourself a multiple orgasm. Researchers suspect that the women most likely to experience a multiple orgasm are the women who know how to build their arousal. The ultimate orgasm—again—is the one that follows the erotic experience you love the most.

Everybody's body works the same way. *Indirectly.* Arousal triggers an involuntary reflex—lubrication. Higher arousal triggers an involuntary neuromuscular reflex—orgasm. All Dorothy has to do is build her arousal. Her body will take care of the rest.

Dorothy is unhappy with this explanation:

> Really, but I don't have any trouble with the . . . getting aroused and all. I love George. I have trouble with two things—a dry vagina and having an orgasm.

Stubbornly ignoring the vastness of her erotic arousal system, Dorothy, like many of us, advances resolutely forward in the wrong direction. While her erotic arousal is barely a consideration, she has the astonishing expectation that her blood will flow to her genitals and stay trapped there.

Wrong expectation.

Biological truth: lubrication and orgasms are involuntary responses to high erotic arousal. Build the arousal, the lubrication and orgasm will follow. Always.

George insists that Dorothy's problem is physical, when he isn't convinced it's psychological:

> There's something really wrong. A sweet young girl like Dorothy . . . and she's so dry. When it comes to sex, you go so far and she turns into a board. Maybe . . . well, I thought about this . . . would it be possible . . . she says, she's always telling me . . . it's not my fault . . . but she distrusts men. Now, if she distrusts men so much she turns her whole body off, how can I fight that?

Actually, Dorothy's problem developed—as many women's do—when she failed to learn the erotic skills that other little girls were learning. She overreacted to her mother's messages about her genitals given during her infant years and in grade school she had some disastrous sex experiences that every female should be spared—and she never recovered.

Two Women: The One Who Orgasms and The One Who Doesn't

Dorothy is shy. She has been shy all her life. She was a shy baby—quiet, neat, well-behaved. Dorothy's mother removed Dorothy's three-year-old baby hands from her genitals and told her daughter in a strikingly serious voice that she was *never* to touch herself *down there* again. Smart little Dorothy, who was always good at following directions, listened closely and never did touch her genitals, not in grade school, not in high school, not in college, not after she had lovers. Never.

Her genitals remained untouched until she was eight.

Lenny was a junior in high school. I've never told anyone this . . . about Lenny. He got a real old used car and he would come to the grade school to pick me up. My Aunt Jean thought she had such a nice little boy. He did something years before that. I was real little, four or five. He called me to see something in his bedroom and he pulled his pants down and ran around and laughed. I was really . . . in shock, I guess . . . I felt . . . I knew this was very bad and that I shouldn't be there.

In the car, he would put one hand in my pants and feel my vagina . . . put his finger all the way in. I was too terrified to tell him to stop . . . or tell him anything. I couldn't say words. I remember . . . I must have been holding my breath . . . it was like when I fell off a swing and had the breath knocked out of me . . . and by the time he let me out I was gasping and I would see things flying through the air . . . and I couldn't believe . . . Sometimes when George touches me I have a flash, like it's Lenny's hands. I felt there was something very bad about me.

141

Eight-year-old Dorothy handled the situation to the best of her ability at the time: she blocked all sensation; she pretended nothing was happening; twice a week for two years.

Through high school, college, her early work years, Dorothy avoided men. She felt shy about being with a boy—being a girl with a boy—so at the hint of an erotic spark, she became invisible. Saying, "Girls who wear tight skimpy clothes are a disgrace and they are just asking for what they get," Dorothy adopted a costume of sweatshirts and loose slacks. Even with her body fairly well disguised, Dorothy was attractive. She was sweet-tempered, kind. Her blond hair was always shiny clean and always sexily just hanging straight to her waist. Although she never flirted, Dorothy smiled. She laughed.

When a boy asked her out she let him manage the erotic side of the relationship. She had no idea what she should do. Beyond saying no. Or saying nothing. Consequently, she did what the guy wanted, and every time she didn't like what he did, she left him. George is lover number five and she is about to leave again. Although she wanted to be with boys—to be courted, be loved, to love them—sex was the complicating factor. Like an animal sensing danger, Dorothy would freeze and then run.

It used to be thought, five years ago, that women who had yet to have an orgasm were the products of repressive parents, repressive religion, or that in their youth they had negative sexual experiences. Large numbers of women who have yet to have an orgasm do report a scenario similar to Dorothy's. They say they feel they are unable to have an orgasm *because* their mothers never talked to them about sex; they were defenseless against an older male relative; they were frightened by religious teaching that sex was a sin. Some researchers wrote that this sensually repressive background was the *cause* of orgasmic failure, until someone thought to ask *orgasmic* women about their backgrounds, expecting to find that they grew up in a sexually unrepressed environment. The surprise was that they also reported having mothers and fathers who never talked to them about sex, older male relatives who victimized them, sensually repressive religious training. What the nonorgasmic women reported, rather than being each woman's *unique* experience, was a cultural phenomenon common to most women.

If nearly every woman has similar experiences, why do some women have difficulty having orgasms?

A new concept: *the susceptible female.* A shy girl, an unassertive girl confronted with the near certainties of sexual passage through her society may fail to develop the natural sexual skills that other women develop.

Dorothy, born with a totally different personality—with a feisty, assertive self—would have turned out differently. If she had been feisty from the beginning—like her friend Marcia—she would, like Marcia, have had an easier time with boys and with sex.

Marcia:

One of my earliest memories . . . my teddy bear, brown eyes with yellow flecks. I would lie on top of my teddy bear to sleep . . . and then put him between my legs. I would rub the bear back and forth, and I remember it was a great feeling . . . really great. Very soothing. I would look forward to it.

I remember the table leg . . . I can see the table leg and my mother's dress . . . little white dots on dark blue. I was under the table rubbing myself with my bear, rocking back and forth, and my mother yanked me out of there. She said I couldn't do that. I remember it so well because my mother never got excited or yelled much and this had a very emotional ingredient . . . very tense . . . it was a grownup acting some way very different and very special like they acted when my grandmother died or the time they turned the car over.

I remember thinking that I could too do it—like she was saying I didn't know how and I was disagreeing. But I never did it in front of any grownups again.

Marcia remembered her mother's "No" all her life. However, it didn't occur to Marcia to stop feeling good; she only stopped in public. In her crib, she and Teddy were inseparable.

I had a friend who would sometimes cry because . . . now this was when she's thirteen . . . boys would feel her up . . . and once this older man did, too . . . on a train. She said she couldn't do anything about it. I could never understand that.

The summer before I went to first grade, a neighbor kid, Billy, going into fifth grade, tried to pull my panties down to see what I had in there . . . anyway, I bet that was the last time he *ever* tried anything like that. I made such a loudmouth fuss, before it was over everybody in the neighborhood had a blow-by-blow description. I ran straight to *his mother*. And then to my mother. And then to my girlfriend's mother. I was like a little old town crier, screaming the news all over the neighborhood: "Billy pinched my butt and I socked him."

Sexually, Marcia was highly visible. She made decisions. As a high-school freshman, she decided she would like a boy to feel her breasts. In her senior year, she decided she would enjoy letting a boy touch her vagina. She had been having orgasms for years and it didn't occur to her that she shouldn't have one with a boy.

> I dated Bucky my senior year. That poor boy . . . I really told him where to put his fingers, how to put his fingers, and when to stop. You know, once he was so shy, but he said I was cool because he could tell me things about how to give him a hand job that he couldn't ever tell any other girl.
>
> I was firm: no intercourse. I was straight on with that. I told him I wasn't going to worry about pregnancy. I wasn't ready for that kind of commitment, and I knew it. Everything we did was great . . . I loved it. But hand jobs, and necking and feeling around over everything, that's all I would do. That was it. Period.

For Marcia there were always orgasms . . . and no conflicts. When she fell madly in love during college she had penis-in-the-vagina intercourse ending in tumultuous orgasms and no conflicts. That relationship didn't work out. Marcia married someone else and had an erotically blissful orgasmic sex life—again without conflicts.

Marcia is so successful because she has developed a skill. But Marcia never thinks of what she does in bed as having anything to do with skill. Starting her genital explorations at two and one-half with not enough thoughts in her baby head to have any expectations, Marcia thinks she does what comes naturally. She is quite puzzled by Dorothy's difficulties. Marcia has always stayed close to her erotic feelings, so close that she cannot imagine how a woman could be *unable* to feel erotic. Marcia worries about keeping her arousal down so she doesn't climax too fast. So does George. He's been having orgasms for so many years by himself and with lovers—and is now so skillful—that he also wouldn't believe that what he does is a skill.

Marcia gives Dorothy advice:
Just be sure when you're with a man you get what you want, hon, that's the important thing.

Very good advice, indeed, except Dorothy's first problem is that she doesn't know what she wants. And her second problem is that she's too shy to ask for it, if she knew what it was.

George gives Dorothy advice:
See a doctor. There's something wrong with your vagina.

Also very good advice. Except, of course, there's nothing wrong with her vagina. Which she discovers when her gynecologist refers her to a physician who specializes in sex therapy.

Female Impotence: Distinguishing Between Physical and Behavioral Causes

All failure to lubricate or have an orgasm is biological. Whatever the cause, whether it is physical or behavioral, female impotence is the failure of a natural body process. The discrimination between a physical or a behavioral cause is more difficult to make because the blood flow that hardens the walls of the vagina is hidden.
Some guidelines:

• If you lubricate or have an orgasm during masturbation or oral sex, your problem is most likely to be behavioral.

- Most purely physical causes are associated with a known disease or surgery, such as total hysterectomy.

- Vaginal infections such as Monilia or Trichomonas, can cause painful intercourse due to dryness in the vagina which is cured along with the infection. However, in many cases, the woman becomes fearful of the pain she now associates with intercourse—and her muscles still tighten against the expectancy of pain with intercourse, causing new pain. While infections, in themselves, do not *cause* permanent lubrication failure, the combination of the woman's expectancy of pain and her withdrawal from sexual activity following treatment for infection *can* have the behavioral effect: insufficient blood flow to the vagina; lubrication failure; no orgasm.

Measuring your natural sleep erections. There is a simple device—a vaginal photoplythysmograph—which a woman can wear while she sleeps in a laboratory to measure the blood flow into her vaginal walls. Smaller than a lipstick case, this device uses photo light cells to measure the amount of blood, and that measurement is then recorded in a polygraph tracing. As with men, most women find their unconscious involuntary erotic systems work perfectly. And, as with men, blood flow is powerfully affected by what each woman *does* with her lover.

If your orgasmic failure is physically caused, *the only* way to determine how much of the physical impairment will be overcome by changing your sex behavior is by changing your sex behavior and looking at what happens.

Five Steps to Having an Orgasm With Him

Her Body for Her, First

1. Find out which thoughts are erotic, which touch arouses.
2. Concentrate solely on building arousal.

Her Body for the Two of Them

3. Tell him which touch excites.
4. Make love with no expectation of lubrication or orgasm.
5. Focus on arousal. The woman controls her lover's touch so she can concentrate solely on feeling her own arousal.

How She Fails

Session 1: Dorothy, like many women who have yet to have an orgasm, wants to concentrate on what she has already experienced: the impossibility of feeling much arousal. Like a butterfly pinned to a block, Dorothy is trapped. She recites all the reasons why her sex life is the way it is and why it is undoubtedly going to stay exactly the same *forever*.

The Chronically Underaroused Woman's Usual Reasons for Staying That Way

1. The problem is I've been shy about sex all my life.
2. The problem is my mother was sexually repressed.
3. The problem is fifteen years ago my cousin molested me so now every time a man puts his hand on me I think of my cousin's hand.
4. The problem is that I have no sexual thoughts, no fantasies. My mind is dead. I have no idea what I could think about if I thought about sexy things. If I have an erotic mind, it's a secret from me.
5. The problem is that I have no idea what I want sexually—my only thought is something general, like a two-hour massage. I never have touched myself and would feel very uncomfortable doing that. My body is a mystery to me.
6. The problem is that my lover doesn't *give* me an orgasm.
7. The problem is that my lover never takes the time to teach me what I might enjoy.
8. The problem is that he has trouble keeping an erection.
9. The problem is that it's *his* fault I don't feel anything.
10. The problem is *he does not want me to feel sexual pleasure*.

Inherent in each "problem" is the same terrible conclusion: *Therefore I can take no responsibility for my body.*

Her first three reasons—her childhood shyness, her mother-child relationship, her third-grade experience with a sexually abusive cousin—put Dorothy in a dilemma. The trouble is each reason is based on a past event. And the trouble with that is that past events are forever. The past never changes. And she can't change it. So as long as Dorothy—or any woman—pins a sex problem on the past, she has a problem for which there is no solution. Ever. Her payoff: I never have to take responsibility for my body. I can stay the same, I can keep feeling nothing forever.

This, of course, is only a little more deadly than her assumption in her last four reasons: This problem with my body is somebody else's fault. Having had such terrible experiences, Dorothy disavows all responsibility for her body. Irrationally, Dorothy hopes that some other person will (and should) take responsibility for her very personal sex life. With her mother living three states away and barely able to speak of the existence of sex, her cousin dead of alcoholism, her previous lovers out of the picture, she focuses on George. She would change her sex behavior, she says, but she can't because of George.

> I don't want to touch myself and find out about my sensuality because I'm not convinced that George wants to know. I feel as though I'm almost fighting with him to tell him anything about me. I have a gut feeling that George will disapprove. He will not stand for my being so selfish as to want to do something for my own frivolous gratification. Anyway, I was sort of saving up my enjoyment time for the weekend with George, but in the summer he's always playing ball on the weekends and too tired to try and do stuff. So I was mad at him. We did have sex four times. He seemed to like it. To me, it was the same as always—I'm just a means to his gratification.

And, she adds, sliding her secret dagger into her lover's heart: "It's all his fault." She finds his touch too fast, too rough, too insensitive. Having decided to block her eroticism, years before she met him, Dorothy has made George helpless. He touches the body of a woman who isn't there. George touches the body of a woman who doesn't know what she feels.

So he is always beyond her. *Before* she will be able to share her body with a lover, Dorothy has to find out what Dorothy enjoys.

Will she *ever* feel comfortable, she wonders. Should she ignore her feelings, she worries. After all, she does *feel* that thinking and touching are wrong; she has had some pretty terrible sexual experiences.

The only way to deal with such a wretched sex history as Dorothy's is to *replace* it. To make a good present history for herself, Dorothy has to do something new. Which means doing something which by its very newness will very likely make her feel uncomfortable. And by its very erotic quality may make her anxious—and reluctant to do it.

If she does change her behavior, she will have an orgasm. And if she doesn't, there are consequences.

The No-Responsibility Circle of Failure

therefore

1 My erotic body and erotic mind are a mystery to me

6 I never have an orgasm

therefore

therefore

2 I have no idea what kinds of sexual stimulation I need before orgasm

5 my lover never gives me the arousal that I need to have an orgasm

besides

therefore

3 even if I knew, I wouldn't tell *him* because I don't think he wants to know.

4 I never teach my lover how to arouse me to orgasm

therefore

To release herself, Dorothy has to do what orgasmic women do—leap over the past and take the five steps to having an orgasm.

149

Her Body for Her, First

Following step 1, Dorothy is to find out which thoughts are erotic, which touch arouses. She is to fantasize exactly how she would like to be touched. She is to think of the erotic options she would most enjoy. She is to touch every inch of her body. She is to find out exactly what touch she likes. Only *after* she feels comfortable touching each part of her body is she to allow George to touch.

The moment Dorothy brings her erotic thoughts into her consciousness, the moment she discovers her own most sensual feelings of touch, she will feel more. The catch: Dorothy finds this action difficult. When the logical part of her brain plans to do the obvious—think erotic thoughts—the anxious, overly emotional part of her brain stalls.

> I've felt very busy and sort of disorganized. I've been trying to set aside time for other things in my life—other things on my list that I've been trying to work through—besides sex. I guess what I'm saying is that I don't value sex. I don't consider sex as important as socializing or going to work or having time to talk things out with George.

At the age of twenty-six, finding out about her sensuality *feels* wrong. It's a new experience. Dorothy feels uncomfortable and awkward. Asked to put herself first—to devote time to her own personal self, to put her entire gratification above every other person's demands on her life—she immediately diverts her thoughts. Dorothy thinks: This isn't right. I've got other priorities.

"I have to take care of other people first." That's delaying action number one, which is followed quickly by delaying actions two, three, and four.

"I would rather have 'real' sex," righteously declares the woman who *has* "real" (penis-in-the-vagina intercourse) sex all the time and dislikes every experience. Behaving as if she had to choose between *only* thinking erotic thoughts and *only* having penis-in-the-vagina intercourse, she shrinks from losing something valuable. But no one is asking Dorothy to give up anything. Dorothy is being asked to do what healthy lovers do, to *add* something valuable to her erotic life.

"And besides, I never have had erotic fantasies. I never have touched myself."

Her Orgasm

If Dorothy never does anything except repeat what she has done, she will never change anything about her life.

Held fast by years of bad sex experiences, Dorothy reinterprets each action that could help her.

Dorothy wants someone else—her friend, her therapist, her lover—to tell her which thoughts are sexy, to tell her which erotic thoughts to think, which touch is most erotic. No good. As Dorothy has said many times, sex is very personal and very private and cannot be learned from a sex manual. Right. Sex is so personal and so private that Dorothy *is* the only one who can think Dorothy's personal, private erotic thoughts. And because of her immense distrust, she is the best person to become sure of her eroticism—first.

But Dorothy claims she can't. In all her conversations Dorothy circles around to the same thought: *". . . and, anyway, George wouldn't like it."* Translation: Sex is bad. Sex is dangerous. Somebody is going to be upset if I do sexual things, and the only person who knows for sure that I do erotic acts is George, so George is going to be angry.

> I would feel, well, disloyal to George. And anyway, this is embarrassing . . . I feel he'll know some way that I'm doing this . . . and, well . . . I already feel he knows something I don't know. He is much more aware of my sexual desires than I am.

George is. George has masturbated for years—he knows exactly how he likes his genitals touched. And he knows the ways he likes the touch to change depending on his level of arousal. And he has touched Dorothy's clitoris and had his fingers in her vagina and his penis in her vagina and touched her breasts and rubbed the inside of her thighs. These actions have given him a certain amount of information—not the specific information that he has about his own genitals, but he knows much more about Dorothy's genitals than Dorothy does. While this may sound deliciously romantic, in Dorothy's real life George is—at best—floundering in the dark. The pressure on George is intense. Although Dorothy lets him determine her sex life, she still wants him to do what makes her feel good. Keeping her wants a secret from him—even, unfortunately, a secret from herself—she watches him struggle, and when he fails she complains that men are only interested in sex for themselves.

George feels he has failed to love her adequately. She feels used.

Impasse.

Thinking your own erotic thoughts, feeling your own erotic body is a skill.
This lack of knowledge about her body puts Dorothy at a disadvantage.
George and she are unequally matched lovers. He is way ahead of her.
George, like 98 percent of men, like nearly every man Dorothy has ever
met, has been thinking erotic thoughts and touching himself to orgasm
for years. And like other men with all this practice, George easily has an
orgasm. Not only that, he brings himself to orgasm all alone nearly every
day—and never sees it as a problem. No feelings of disloyalty to Dorothy.
No worries that she'll know. No concerns that what he does by himself
will have an effect on their sex life. No thought that what he does alone
has anything to do with what he does with Dorothy. He could never
imagine how Dorothy struggles with herself.

Dorothy:
I felt absolutely dumb and ridiculous and never did get past some
feeling that I shouldn't be doing such a thing. I unplugged the
phone, pulled the blinds. I took a long hot shower, really long,
then . . . I never thought of this before . . . but I decided rock music
might add something. I put on the headphones. And . . . I used
baby oil.

For the first time in her life Dorothy labels her eroticism. She tells herself what she likes. She connects her sexual fantasies to her sexual body.

I like the feel of my fingers near my nipples, circling my nipples.
I like the feel of my fingers in my bellybutton. I like the feel of my
fingers on my eyelid. My clitoris is sensitive. My vagina is less sensitive. The right side of my vagina is less sensitive than the left. The
area near the entrance is more sensitive than deeper inside. I like to
feel fingers circling my clitoris—with slow, soft pressure. Hands
directly on my clitoris are unpleasant. My vagina is less sensitive
than I had ever imagined. On the right side halfway in I feel numb.
When George's penis is in my vagina and he leans to the right, I
feel nothing.
When I thought, I must give myself pleasure or suffer the consequence; my lover demands I give him everything, my body reacted

152

much faster to tactile stimulation. My skin flushed. My muscles tightened. My nipples became erect.

I was—I felt foolish. I felt—at first—as though touching myself was foolish and superfluous. As I began to find differences, I became curious. I felt strange to be discovering my own body. Like a scientist—

She Takes Seven Small Actions to Build Her Arousal

1. She touches herself.
2. She puts herself first for two hours.
3. She selects oil as a sensual medium.
4. She chooses a shower as more sensual than a bath—lingering (past her usual sanitary seven minutes) to feel the water against her body.
5. She thinks about what she could add to her environment to heighten her sensuality—rock music heard through the powerful isolation of headphones. Darkness.
6. She thinks erotic thoughts; she feels more aroused.
7. She distinguishes two aspects of caress that she enjoys: lots of skin touching skin, and very light touching.

Now Dorothy knows two things about what she enjoys—and she can tell her lover: "Let me feel a lot of your skin touching me. Touch me lightly."

Dorothy is fantastic. To do so much in two hours after a lifetime of bad sex is nearly unbelievable. The woman who has felt nothing now feels something. Hurrah.

Reactive Worries

But Dorothy is disappointed. She wanted to do more than *begin* to feel; she wanted fireworks. Secretly she had hoped—as she secretly hopes every time she goes to bed with George—that this might be the time she would have an orgasm. Actually, Dorothy has no conception of how much arousal her body needs before her body *will* orgasm. She is innocently unaware of how far away she is.

I did what I was supposed to, but I didn't feel *that much*. I felt as though I was just doing this by prescription. To be honest, there was nothing spontaneous about it.

Dorothy is right. Such a "touch myself" assignment is mechanical. It is by prescription. And she should expect to feel awkward at first, as she would learning any new skill. Like tennis: if you start as an adult, the first few times you will feel awkward, the tennis racquet will feel strange in your hand, you will feel you are just moving around by rote, you will feel you are doing everything because the teacher said to do it, you will feel you never spontaneously sent the ball soaring like a tennis pro.

Now I did like the shower and I did enjoy the music, but every time I put my hand on my body I would hear voices in my head— distracting voices—my mother, not even talking about sex, just there giving me directions about something, George's voice. I would see images of mean boys. I started the record again a couple of times. The music helps me to be alone.

Dorothy, in fact, was more successful than many women with her problem. She was able to discriminate the subtleties of erotic feeling in her genitals, while many women as they finger their genitals for the first time feel nothing. Feeling nothing sends them into a panic:

I'm afraid if I do this nothing is going to happen. I'm afraid I'm dead down there. If I am dead, I don't want to find that out.

This is normal. It is to be expected. A woman who has felt prohibited from touching her own body may not be very good at doing that. The first time she tries to become aware, she may continue to feel little sensitivity. To regain long-denied sensitivity takes time. Going slow is important.

Even Dorothy, as successful as she is, has rushed too far ahead of herself. She worries, *Should* I give myself an orgasm? *Can* I give myself an orgasm? Is my body even *capable* of having an orgasm?

Needless worry. No woman can make herself have an orgasm. The only power any woman has is to build her arousal. The orgasm happens

154

all by itself naturally—once the person has built arousal high enough. An orgasm is a reflex action. No one can make her vaginal muscles contract every .8 second. The only thing Dorothy can do is build her arousal. Dorothy is doing that. She has chosen seven actions to build her arousal. She is on the right track. She feels the glimmers of eroticism. If she continues, she will succeed.

She does just what she should do. She proceeds to step 2.

The second step—concentrating solely on building arousal—lasts through Dorothy's next four sessions.

> I feel a little more each time. I think about George doing sexy things to me. George sliding his erect penis along my spine. George putting his erect penis between my buttocks. George sliding his penis over my clitoris. George penetrating my vagina, holding his penis perfectly still while I beg for more. I push myself into him, pull against him.
>
> I imagine myself saying, "Hard nipples, George. Sexy lady, George. Hot pussy, George."

Vibrators

> I took it out of the bureau—looked at the penis-shaped thing—and broke into tears. My past comes flooding in on me. Why am I doing this? I am not the kind of person who does this. I don't *want* a stupid machine. I want a lover and a love affair.

Sex therapists sometimes do recommend that women who have yet to experience high arousal use a vibrator. For many women this technique has helped. Vibrators do increase arousal. For men and women. Vibrators are not for everybody. Neither are they essential. They are only one option that helps some people build arousal.

There are two kinds. One fits on the back of the hand and sends vibrations through the fingers. The second is applied directly to the body. Unfortunately, one variation of this second type is shaped like a penis. It is not a penis substitute. It does *not* go in the vagina. It is to be used to increase general stimulation to the body and to the area around the clito-

ris. Often it is used—like the first—to increase the hand's vibrations.
Both can be used with a lover.

> It was a mistake. With the vibrator, well, you know ... I had a
> wrong conception of what it was and what it was going to do. I
> thought it was going to be a replacement for a penis, which it is
> not, and I thought it was going to give a heavy feeling, which it
> doesn't. When I just felt the vibrations, like a relaxing massage, I
> had to change my idea on how I was going to use it. I ran it over
> my inner thighs, up and around my clit, back to my thigh, up and
> around my nipples, then around and around my clit.

Fear of Letting Go

Odd. Dorothy is floating sensually along—blocking out her past—
thinking erotic thoughts, enjoying erotic touch ... when she stops. She
cannot go on. She is so close to letting go—but she can't. She fears losing
control. "What if," she worries, "what if I lose control and something
terrible happens. What if I build higher and higher and nothing happens?"

Those are the only two things that *can* happen—either she will lose
control and have an orgasm or she will be unable to lose control.
Dorothy is nervous about either possibility.

Playacting is the answer to the fear of losing control. What is the
worst thing you would do if you lost control? Writhe around? Make
noise? Pant? Cry? You're alone. Do it. Writhe. Yell. Pant. Cry.

Dorothy fears she will jerk around. She fears she will leave vaginal
drippings on the sheets. So she practices. She jerks, she drops baby oil on
the sheets. Nothing bad happens. She feels better.

How should she handle the alternative: What if she's dead down
there? What if she feels more and more aroused and nothing happens?
Even if she finds out that she is the rare woman who is physically impaired, Dorothy still has to find out *where* she is erotically sensitive, *how*
she is erotically sensitive, and *what* erotic touch she does like.

Either way, it is essential to Dorothy that she find out every erotic
thing about Dorothy.

Finding Out Every Erotic Thing

I had just finished lesson plans for all five third grades, and I was feeling good. I turned out all the lights, lay down on the bed, put on the headphones. I was tense. It had been a long time since I tried . . . well, I guess I had regressed. I had to start the record over again because the voices kept creeping in. I had to put a real effort into, you know, trying not to think about what George would say. I would hear other people's voices, and whenever I did, I made myself concentrate on the music. When I hear the voices my sexual energy, you know . . . it just goes real down. I would isolate myself with the music; the energy would return. The energy fluctuated . . . that was noticeable . . . I find I have little sexual energy . . . until I get rid of everybody else . . . the music, well, it stops me from thinking. It fills my head with something, something not coming from me, coming from somewhere else. I concentrate on the sound. I guess I am trying, really, not to worry about having an orgasm.

I touch myself very lightly with my fingers and sometimes with the vibrator. The area around the base of my clitoris is the nicest. Sometimes I want more pressure. When I start to get very excited, I use my full hand and rub with very firm pressure. The movement isn't a conscious pattern. I don't think: Move your hands, here or there. I just wait. I respond to the music. The music gets more exciting, I move my hands in rhythm.

I am exciting myself very lightly, and as I start to get very excited I use my full hand, pressing firmly back and forth, up and down, around my clitoris. At the same time my back arches and I feel very warm. The muscles in my legs are hard and tight. I am breathing faster. Faster. Faster. Faster. I feel exhausted. I just lie back, listen to the music. I touch myself and then the same thing happens, my back arches, my muscles tense. The second time it isn't as strong and doesn't last as long. After that, I touch myself very, very lightly, sort of calming myself to sleep. I am tired. Just calming myself, feeling nice.

Orgasm. Orgasm. Orgasm. Hurrah! Hurrah!

How She Misses Out on Her Lover's Help

Dorothy is astonished. Well, for one thing, she had imagined the path to her orgasm was going to be a mirror image of George's. He would stroke in, she would pull out—faster, faster, eureka, orgasm. But now she has discovered that everything she needs to get excited is completely different from what he needs.

What She Likes But Can't Tell Him

What Dorothy Likes	What George Likes
1. To be in her own bed.	1. To be in his own bed.
2. To be relaxed from a long shower.	2. To get right to penetration.
3. To have the lights out.	3. Lights on.
4. To have her mind filled with hard-rock music.	4. Silence.
5. To be oiled up and slicked down.	5. Dry skin.
6. To think about how sexy she is to George, how he wants her, and she keeps herself slightly away, until he begs.	6. To think about what they are going to do next.
7. To touch herself, slowly, rhythmically around her breasts, down her belly, rhythmically on her clitoris, back and forth, same motion over and over, adding the vibrator around the clitoris.	7. To thrust faster and faster feeling the incredibly arousing feel of her vagina against his penis.
8. To break rhythm, stop, start over.	8. To thrust hard and fast and straight to the goal—ejaculation.

Dorothy complains:

> We even want different rhythms. There is *no way* to get these
> two sets of needs together.

Her new dilemma: She has all this information about her erotic
needs—but what is she to do with it? She certainly can't tell George.
Which makes him . . .

Choosing the Worst Possible Lover

In bed, he's a take-charge guy. He believes, in the traditional male way,
what he has been taught to believe about sex since he was a boy: the man
knows the answer; the woman doesn't know the answer; the answer is
climax.

Dorothy has had other lovers, but the others have been from the same
mold. In truth, Dorothy always goes for guys who are just like George in
bed. Such a man is terribly attractive to a sexually shy woman. He was
the perfect match when 1) she didn't want to tell a man anything about
her sexual arousal, and 2) she didn't have anything to tell.

However, the situation has changed. George is making love to a
woman who has orgasms. Only he doesn't know it. Dorothy can't tell
him. It's tough to tell him the tiniest thing because he is so sure he already knows the answer.

He knows the answer. George has been taught that men do. A real man
knows everything about sex—or should—believes George.

> I've educated myself. Would you believe I've got a little stack of
> sex books hidden away. Let's see . . . I've read *The Joy of Sex* and *The
> Kama Sutra*. I know more sexual positions than I'll ever use. Espe-
> cially if I marry Dorothy. I pay close attention to what feels good
> to me and I figure if Dorothy would just relax what I like would
> feel good to her, too.

And then, George reveals the secret that's been bothering him:

Would you believe I'm battling—with this. I slept with two women before Dorothy and both of them seemed so uninterested in sex. I guess women are just not as interested in sex as men.

Wrong guess. Women are exactly as sexual as men—*if* they develop their sexuality. And *if* they do with their lovers what feels good to a woman.

George believes women are less interested in sex because that's what women have told him. They've also led him to believe that what feels good to him will also feel good to them—or should. When he touches them the way *he* likes, the women he has made love to—so sexually shy they are barely aware of what arouses them—have told George:

It was fine. Really, George. Really great. I guess I'm just not as sexual as you.

Which leads George to say:

The sexes are different. I've always known *that*. Women are not as sexual as men. That's the difference.

The difference is, of course, that men and women have very different sensitivity in their sexual bodies. Although George, because of his great love for Dorothy, struggles to please her, he never does. Operating within the idea that doing everything in bed his way is the natural way to make love, he has to fail. For George sex is a very tricky business because he does do nearly everything he can think of to please her—*within his cultural boundaries.* Of course, giving her what she needs in the order she needs it is out of bounds. He can't do that because he can't ask her. Why? Because he believes he already knows the answer. And . . .

She doesn't know the answer. Women don't. So why listen? In Dorothy's case, George has proof. Dreamily Dorothy has talked of his giving her a two-hour massage. She has told him she hurts . . . told him her vagina is insensitive . . . told him they really have to talk. He figures this has to be useless information because none of it seems to have anything to do with having an orgasm.

And . . .

The answer is climax. But when he touches her vagina, she protests:

160

Her Orgasm

"Do you have to start there so fast?" She feels he is pushing her and poking her. He feels she probably doesn't have an orgasm because she doesn't allow him to get to her cunt as hard and rough as she needs. Raised to take all responsibility for sex, George expects that it is his job to give Dorothy an orgasm. He can't. And when he works hard to make her come, everything he does lowers her arousal. And his. Still, George figures, any day now, if he just keeps forcing the situation, Dorothy *will* climax. Dorothy sees this as such a ghastly expectation that she wants to get away from him—at least get away from having sex with him.

Trust is the most important sex act. To have an orgasm with George, Dorothy needs to trust him.

George agrees that trust is important:

> I've told Dorothy to trust me . . . told her over and over till I'm blue in the face. She tells me she can't. She says she distrusts men and has since she was in grade school. I love Dorothy. I'm the one guy she *can* trust, but she isn't going to trust me or any guy when it comes to sex.

Part of what George says is correct, Dorothy will never trust George just because he says, "Trust me." As long as he unintentionally hurts her during intercourse and she can't tell him so he can stop, they have no way of trusting each other. And, as long as they do everything his way so she is always left out and she keeps saying, "You're a great lover, everything you do is fine," they have no way of trusting each other.

Trust is built of small pieces. Dorothy can learn to trust George. As a lover, George can gain her trust rather simply. The secret learned from the sex therapists: trust *follows* her lover's doing what she asks him to do.

George:
> That's fine, but Dorothy never asks for anything—well, once she asked for a massage and I rubbed her back, but it wasn't very sexy.

And he's right again. Which is why sex therapy has evolved a system that helps Dorothy tell him what she wants in small steps designed to start at a comfortable place for her and to go forward until the lovers discover a vast repertoire of erotic acts they can share.

161

Her Body for the Two of Them:
How She Tells Him What She Wants

The therapist tells Dorothy to do one thing with her lover. She is to follow step 3: tell him which touch excites. The easiest way to do that is to add the support of step 4: make love with no expectation of lubrication or orgasm. That step frees the lovers to discover Dorothy's body with no pressure to perform. After they define their goal as discovery, they are to add the specific help of step 5: focus on arousal. The woman—temporarily—controls her lover's touch so she can concentrate solely on feeling her own arousal.

Privately, George agrees to follow these last three steps, but it is Dorothy who stubbornly refuses. To have sex this way, even for a short time, smashes her dearly held lifelong belief that sex is for men. Negative thoughts spring into her mind like little red signs.

> I don't know if I should say this is what I want. And I am ashamed a little bit.

The problem:
If Dorothy doesn't tell him what she wants, who is going to tell him?

> But, I don't want to say, I want this, I want this. He doesn't initiate. What am I supposed to do—beg for what I want?

The problem:
Dorothy has gotten so emotional, she magnifies the act of sharing her erotic secrets with her lover. Giving information to her lover—suddenly becomes *begging*.
Dorothy's question:
"How do I know he wants to give this to me?"

There are two answers to this crucial question.

1. He won't want to give erotic pleasure to you if he doesn't know what to do, because he'll be afraid of failing; and, of course, he will fail if you never tell him anything about your needs.
2. If, in fact, he refuses to touch you to give you pleasure—if he refuses to "just please Dorothy" even once—then you know something *very* important. You know he has no interest in your feeling anything. Then what? You would know you should dump him. No one wants a lover who doesn't care enough about her to touch her. The whole point of being lovers is that both of you do care.

With these two thoughts in mind, Dorothy begins.

Touching Her More

Session 1: Dorothy is to tell George how she wants him to touch each part of her body. She is to keep the touch of discovery separate from penis-in-the-vagina intercourse. The biggest struggle of their short sex lives has centered on Dorothy's genitals. Talking about genitals is not the place to start.

> George, please touch me more. I want to feel your hands on me, I want to feel your warm skin next to mine. Touch me more. Touch me lightly.

George does.

Dorothy is astonished:
> It used to go like this: We'd lie against each other in bed. I'd rub his chest and touch his face because I like to touch him. I always wished he'd do the same to me, but he never did. Then in the last couple of nights he'd touch me, this morning he was touching me. That's something he's never done before. The last two or three days he's been touching me all the time. I don't know why he's so overly affectionate.

There is an immediate cause-and-effect here. Dorothy says touch me more; her lover touches her; she feels loved.

Anyone can see that. Except Dorothy. Dorothy is puzzled. She has a weak notion of erotic cause-and-effect. Never in her life has she asked a man to do sexual acts she wanted; therefore a man has never responded to her desires. When he does she erroneously starts looking for *other* reasons: "He's getting a cold; he's got trouble at work."

Wrong place to look.

George touches Dorothy *only* because Dorothy *asked* him to touch her. The credit is hers. She made it happen. She has to accept her power.

Their relationship has changed. George gave Dorothy what she asked for. That act has great impact. She trusts him the tiniest bit—just enough to haltingly reveal one more sexual secret.

Session 2: Tell your lover which *exact* touch you prefer. One part of your body at a time. No penetration. No orgasm. Concentrate fully on feeling your eroticism. For half an hour.

Dorothy loves George; she wants to feel his hands on her body. It's important to say that in the most positively reassuring manner.

> *Best opening speech:* "I love to be close to you. I love to make love to you, George—but I need to slow down to find out what feels good to me. I need your help. I want to spend half an hour to feel your hands on me and feel which touch feels more pleasurable. I am so tired of trying to have an orgasm. I get so anxious about trying. I stop feeling. I don't want to do that. I want to feel my connection with you. I love you."

> *Best position:* Dorothy sits naked in front of George, between his legs, with her back against his chest. He can touch her everywhere. Neither lover feels pressured to perform. No expectancy of penis-in-the-vagina intercourse for George. No expectancy for Dorothy that she has to do anything more than feel. The lovers are to start where Dorothy is.

They do. And, considering their past history, Dorothy's reluctance to trust and George's inexperience with giving erotic touch, they are incredibly successful. George touches Dorothy. She guides him.

> If there was something I thought he could do to make me feel good that was really easy, I would tell him. I would hold his hand on my body in a certain place. Or I would say touch me more

slowly. Or more lightly. Or if he did something on his own that I liked, I would say I like that. And he did touch me different ways . . . well, you know . . . for an hour.

Dorothy underestimates her success.

Fact: She asks her lover to touch her body just for her. He does. *For one hour.*

One hour is an extraordinarily long time for someone with George's sex history to be able to touch a lover. What accounted for this drastic change in his ability to sustain this tender touching of Dorothy? Dorothy. Dorothy, who had wished for a perfect fantasy lover to take over her sexual life and relieve her of her anxiety, has a lover who—like most lovers—has sexual anxiety of his own. Faced with a new way to be erotic, George expresses his anxiety for the first fifteen minutes with a running commentary:

- This is weird.
- I don't imagine there are a whole lot of couples sitting around on their beds all day doing this.
- I knew it. I knew you didn't like to fuck.
- So this is it, this is what you want to get me doing the rest of my life, instead of fucking.
- You have to admit, this is fucking weird.

She faces his anxiety. She reassures him. Which is why he is able to do what he clearly wants to do—overcome his anxiety and please her for a long time. It is a greater success for Dorothy than she knows. Like many women in her position, Dorothy is highly sensitive to the slightest negative reaction from her lover. Her trust is a small trust. In the past, Dorothy would have closed down all sensual feeling; she would have lain on the bed like a board. But Dorothy changed. *Dorothy faced her lover's anxiety.*

> You are right, George. This is artificial. I need to feel you closer. I need to feel my body reacting to your touch. You know I've been too distant. I need these changes to be a better lover.

Dorothy gives George something. Her way of talking about sex is an excellent model for him to follow. She gives him permission to give her what she needs.

The lovers have had the greatest sexual success of their lives. Dorothy is so incredibly successful, she should be nearly jumping out of her skin with happiness.

But rather than applauding herself and George for doing new actions that bring them closer together, Dorothy worries about *how well* they did the new actions.

> Well, you know, he did it, but he was reluctant. It wasn't very successful for me. What it turned out to be . . . well, he more or less just gave me a massage, which turned out not to be all that helpful. And he was . . . I mean, he couldn't communicate. He didn't *ask* me anything. I could have told him a lot if he would have asked. I'm shy, though. So we didn't get very far. A couple of times, I did say, "I like that."

Fact: The lovers—with all their anxiety—have made a phenomenal change in their erotic relationship.

George did everything Dorothy asked. His hands felt good. The lovers are successful in three important ways.

1. *Dorothy told her lover what she liked.* For the first time in her life, Dorothy told a man: "Touch me here." She said, "I need."
   I need no penis-in-the-vagina intercourse.
   I need your hands on my body.
   I need time.
   I need to feel.
2. *George said yes.* Every single thing she asked for, he tried to give her. This was a first time in his life experience so, as could be expected, he wasn't very good at it. But he did change:
   George asked nothing for himself.
   George kept his hands on her body.
   George tried.
3. *Dorothy was a positive model for her lover.* Concentrating on Dorothy was so difficult for George that he covered up his anxiety with a string of nervous comments, which she faced *and* gave him permission to calm his anxiety and be positive about the touching experience in the same way she was positive.

Her Orgasm

Concern about *how well* she and George are touching is superfluous. They have years to practice touching well. The important thing is that they *are* touching.

Dorothy has yet to completely trust George. However, she does trust him enough to tell him she wants to feel his hands sliding over her oiled body, she wants to feel one of his hands on each of her inner thighs, gently separating her legs, caressing slowly, slightly, higher, higher, higher. The trust and the distrust exist simultaneously in Dorothy, but each act George performs to please her *reassures* her so that she is able to tell him yet another secret. Each secret revealed, and acted upon, builds Dorothy's arousal. George excites Dorothy.

Sitting naked between George's legs, she puts his hand on her hand. She tells him how to trail his fingers over her palm, how to slide deliciously over the inside of her elbow, slide through the slick oily lotion she gives him to coat her body, around her navel, three fingers on her inner thighs, rolling her over, smooth palms down the back of her calves, each hand up on each inner thigh, lightly up, up, up, slowly, lightly up, up, up, slowly, lightly almost to her genitals.

A gargantuan leap: Dorothy no longer feels used. And George has a lover who is aroused by his touch.

So far, so good.

About Her Clitoris

Session 3: Although Dorothy has made great advances, she is shy.

> I asked him to touch my cunt—I still can't get used to that word—that's George's word. I couldn't tell him *specific* things. I couldn't show him anything I wanted him to do. I was too embarrassed. I can't because, I mean, I know he doesn't want to touch my clit.

Silent Dorothy leaves her lover stranded. Every time Dorothy tries to tell him how to touch her genitals, she fails because, quite simply, she gives him the wrong information.

I try to teach him that my body is just like his. It seems to me he has trouble seeing that. Believe me, I've tried. If he handles my breasts too roughly and I tell him that's too painful, I always say that if I did that to your balls it would hurt, too, because they're probably about equally sensitive. Or if I say, when you touch me on my clit it's like when I touch you on your penis, he just doesn't seem to see the connection, to see that it makes me feel like it makes him feel. He touches me too rough. Too fast. He doesn't seem to be able to have that empathic connection with a woman's body.

Wrong thing to teach.

George shouldn't be expected to have an empathic connection to a female body. His body is *not* just like hers. Breasts are *not* just like testicles. And, although the clitoris and the penis are erotic equivalents, they are radically different in sensitivity. George does exactly what Dorothy suggests: he touches her clitoris just as he would want his penis touched—hard, fast, and rough. She hates it.

Using this experience as their frame of reference, the lovers are reluctant to believe that they can build Dorothy's arousal high enough for her to orgasm.

Dorothy:

He is getting quite good at touching my body. It feels so pleasant now. But, I mean, I don't feel at all like I'm going to have an orgasm. When it comes to my vagina and clitoris, I'm just not convinced that he *can* make me feel good enough.

George:

I've always felt that there is no way a man can learn the intimate details of what a woman feels through her clitoris or vagina. It is easy for her. She feels the sensation the instant she touches herself and she can modify instantly. There is such a fine line between what feels good and what is too stimulating, and I've always felt there was no way I could learn that. I had this girlfriend who put my hand right on her spare tongue . . . right there above her vagina . . . and a couple of times when I took my hand away, she put it back, but I still had only a general impression. I could never tell if she liked the place I was touching or the pressure I was using or the rhythm or what.

Exploring His Lover's Vagina

Session 4: The lovers proceed. George touches Dorothy's genitals inside her vagina, outside her vagina, on her clitoris, around her clitoris. Dorothy tells him what she feels, her lover is astonished.

George reports:

I've thought sometimes that my penis might be too small or too short ... I touched her vagina as far in as I could, thinking she'd get real excited ... would you believe on the inner third she feels just about nothing? That was a shock. She liked the feel of two fingers and really liked the sensation of touch right inside the opening of her cunt ... of her vagina ... seemed to like the outer third at about five o'clock more ... but not that much more.

The thing I can't get over is she likes her clitoris touched best ... no comparison ... she was moaning and carrying on so I got so excited ... I really wanted to fuck her brains out ... would you believe this is her greatest pleasure and my penis doesn't even touch her there.

Dorothy calms her lover's *fears:*

I love you. I love the feel of you inside me. George, I will always want to feel your penis in my vagina. That makes me feel complete and wonderful. I love having sex with you so much I want to feel every good feeling I can on every part of my body.

Hold me close. That feels good. Put your hands on my breasts. Your hands feel warm. I love that. Your hands just there on my breasts. Quite still.

Dorothy sighs. She moves his hands to her genitals. Inside her vagina. Around her clitoris. Dorothy has a lovely sensual experience, but her lover worries.

There is no "instant feedback" from her clitoris to my fingers. I'm impatient.

She placed my fingers just as she wanted them and said, "Softer." I learned that the pressure had to be softer than I would have imagined (much softer than I would ever like on my penis) and the speed faster. Dorothy likes a repetitive motion. The first couple of times she told me this, I got bored so I changed the motion. When I did, her arousal dropped. It's a dumb motion, I think, boring . . . nothing I would like really. But when I touch her just like she says, she gets so hot . . . I can't believe the way she acts . . . my shy little Dorothy . . . she's the sexiest woman.

George has now learned the most valuable sexual information he can ever learn about Dorothy—she wants her lover to touch her clitoris lightly and swiftly with the same motion.

That's the trouble, my mind keeps filling up with what makes me feel good and I get impatient. I want touching her cunt to be fast and easy like when I touch my penis.

It is still hard for me to believe. I think of myself and I think penis; the counterpart of that is vagina.

I have spent all my life believing that a woman's vagina is as sensitive as my penis. Thinking that it was my penis that gave her the most pleasure. I am not illiterate. I read sex books. I have read *The Hite Report* and Masters and Johnson, so I know about the percentages, that most women say they need clitoral stimulation to have an orgasm and I know Dorothy never had an orgasm before she started touching herself. That—right there—is a mind-blower. I find out Dorothy has orgasms. But not with me.

I cannot help it, I feel—*feel,* which is different from know—that some way it still should be the way I've always been told, that penis against vagina is the highest erotic sensation for lovers. For me it is. And I *feel* it is for her—or it should be.

And then I feel she should be able to get hot faster. By myself I can jerk off in two minutes. Easy. It's fast. I'm getting that instantaneous feedback. I'm real good at it.

I resent not having that advantage with her body. Her body gets excited *so* slow. Also I'm working in the dark. The only way I know is to let her tell me.

There is something in me that just wants to do it *my* way. I got finally convinced that Dorothy knows. I mean, when I touch her body the way she tells me she gets so hot I can hardly stand it.

Session 5: Dorothy describes an erotic experience that is light years away from the painful intercourse of two months ago:

This morning I told him that I missed his touch. He came back to bed. We talked for a little while. He lay on his side. He held me between his legs with my back to him. He caressed my face, started to rub my breasts, and to stimulate me on my clit. His hands felt very nice. He did this for some time, while I just lay there and let him do it. I didn't touch him. I had my body against his, so I was touching him that way, but I didn't touch him with my fingers, which was different for me. Feeling the attention, feeling his hands. I started to float. I felt the heat of his body. I felt myself slide into him. I felt myself so open to his touch. I felt so hot, so excited . . . so wanting.

They have had trouble in the past because of what they didn't know. He would touch her. She would feel nothing. She wouldn't tell him. He wouldn't know.

George:

I feel as though a weight has been lifted from my shoulders.

It is such a simple thing to find out. It is erotic here. Not here.

I have touched her breasts just the way she said would arouse her the most and I could tell by her muscle tension, by her moans, by the heavy lubrication flowing from her vagina that this was a sensual high for her. I have touched her clitoris working with her to discover subtleties of caress that would give her the greatest pleasure. And I have touched her vagina—slowly, feeling very close to her, very warm, very sensual, looking into her eyes, feeling her love, and I found irrevocable information that this woman, my lover, is the most erotic creature I've ever been near.

His Body for Her

Session 6: Using each long-hidden bit of erotic information, he excites her more.

Dorothy:

George, give me your hand. When you put your hand here like this yesterday morning it felt so good. Here, let me lace my fingers with yours. Right here above the clitoris, that feels good. A bit lighter. Yes. Exactly.

Dorothy puts his erect penis inside her vagina. She feels one thing: his penis. His penis for her erotic feeling. His penis inside her. Perfectly still. Her cunt reaching to feel more.

A new concept: His body for her. His penis for her.

Dorothy has made so many changes and now she *feels* different:

I love George. I mean ... you know ... I've always loved George. But now I feel so hopeful. I trust him. That's why I can tell him so many things about my body that I've never been able to tell anyone. I feel this is just the beginning.

And it is.

Her Most Important Sex Act: Trust

Session 7: She runs her fingers along his chest, down his body, up and down his thighs, trails her fingers in loops through his pubic hair.

He rubs her body with oil, licks her clitoris. Again. Again. Caresses back and forth over the base of the clitoris with two fingers the way she has taught him. She moans. He runs his fingers around and around the edges of her mouth, in her mouth, and out. Around and around her vagina, into her vagina and out.

Dorothy plays with his erect penis. She rolls on top of him and puts his penis in her vagina, slowly feeling each bit of erect penis against her vaginal walls. She waits. Feels the still, erect penis within her. Dorothy raises her body, lowers it, clutches the penis within her, begins slow thrusting. Feels. Thrusts her vagina up and down faster over her lover's penis. She feels erotic. She hugs her lover. Kisses her lover. She slips away from his penis. Relaxes. She rubs her body against his. Places his fingers on her clitoris. Feels his fingers. After a while she wants to feel his penis inside her again. She puts his penis in her vagina. Feels his penis. She is isolated with her bodily sensations. She feels tension building in her body. She thinks of when she is alone. Of her music, of her lusting fantasies of George.

He thrusts. He moves his fingers over her clitoris, back and forth, the repetitions arousing her higher.

She breathes faster. Her muscles tighten. Her back arches. She comes. Comes. Comes. Orgasm. Orgasm. Orgasm. Hurrah! George, exicted by his amorous, sexy, sexy lover, has been holding back. Now he thrusts, thrusts, thrusts and comes.

They lie in each other's arms. Close.

George: "I love you."

Dorothy: "I love you."

Together. Lovers.

OVERCOMING PREMATURE EJACULATION
Secrets of the Man Who Can Last as Long as He Wants

She was trying to force her tongue into my mouth. Would you believe, I was blocking her tongue with my teeth. Every thing she did made me frantic. I was saying to myself, Hold on. Don't come. Don't come. She rubbed her body against my hard-on. I backed away. I was sweating. I kept my left palm out of her sight and dug my nails into the skin. When she took hold of my dick, I dug into my skin harder. She started to shove it into her. Would you believe, I went into rotten garbage. Real sexy stuff: I thought of rotting garbage, piles of slimy, slushy garbage, huge hairy rats crawling through it. She was fooling around, moving my dick around over her pussy. I was praying, Let me get into her before I come. Garbage. Pain. But it was no use. I came all over her . . . all over the bed, for Christ's sake. There was semen on the wallpaper.

Lover to Lover

What Charles describes is his experience with Susan. Susan is the woman he loved after his divorce.

Yesterday I caught myself saying, "My wife something or other." I can't help it. I think the word *wife* and I think Diane. Would you believe there have been only two women ... in my whole life ... two women that I cared so much about I would do anything to keep from coming so fast. Diane was the first girl ... that, well, I knew my body did this weird thing ... went off like a rocket. And when I met her she was eighteen.

From the day I met Diane, I wanted to make love to her. But I was afraid. She was shy. I liked that. Actually, I felt relieved. I was afraid to try to go all the way with her. Date after date, we would just make out. I kissed her, I put my tongue in her mouth, I would feel her up, feel her breasts through her clothes. I got to the point I was feeling naked breasts, kissing them. I slid my hands up her skirt. She always stopped me outside her panties. I never let her get near my penis.

Would you believe I was terrified I would come in my pants. I did. Twice. The first time I went crazy. I figured this shy little girl would never go for this, so I did the most insane thing to hide it. We were in this old green Chevy I had. So get this ... I faked an allergy attack, went roaring up to a bus stop and pushed her out. I was sort of gasping and yelling that I had to rush to the hospital. I kept gasping ... and wheezing ... emergency room ... emergency room ... allergy ... hospital.

Diane accepted my running the show. She never seemed to notice anything strange. She believed me ... I think she really went for it when I told her I respected her too much to try anything before the wedding.

Would you believe, I discovered a new trick. I started jerking off a couple of times before I would see her so I'd be less tempted to get into something with her. I don't understand how it worked, but all I know, if I jerked off, I could make out without coming. The day we got married I was nervous for more than the usual reasons. So I jerked off a couple times before the ceremony, once after, once that night in the hotel. And that first night I lasted ... after penetrating ... at least four minutes. I was triumphant, ecstatic.

176

His brand-new wife was beautiful to Charles, who swooned at the thought of her tiny breasts, big hips, matronly thighs, and high giggle of a laugh. He adored her. She adored him. But there were things about himself he was afraid to tell.

> I have so many tricks. Sex has come to be . . . would you believe . . . one trick after another.

But his tricks don't work. Six months into his marriage he is coming in less than a minute. By their first anniversary, he is lasting barely thirty seconds. Ironically, he comes too fast because of some other tricks he taught himself years ago when he was a teenager.

Charles's most vivid memory of being fourteen was the moment his mother came into his room carrying a pile of clean sheets and surprised him "jacking off." In a total panic, he screamed in a high, girlish voice, "Get out! Get out of here."

Charles has no idea what his mother thought of what she saw, because they lived out their days together pretending it had never happened. However, Charles remembered every tiny detail of the incident for the rest of his life. Before the incident, he had been like many other boys his age. He stretched out the time from when he started to stimulate himself until he had an orgasm. That period, Charles's *latency to ejaculation,* was fifteen to twenty minutes. But after the incident, Charles changed. In a few months Charles taught himself to masturbate to orgasm in less than ninety seconds. He put in a lot of practice at coming quickly. Soon he was very good. Charles would never be caught again.

A lot of hard work went into Charles's remarkable reduction of his latency. In his teenage years, he brought forth a whole bag of tricks to help him "get off" faster than anyone in his class. He worked on his erotic fantasies, refined them until they were dramatically erotic. Every few months he would change the fantasies, refine them as he stared lustfully at the glossy naked women in *Playboy.* Every few months he changed the naked women. And he developed certain ways of varying the touch of his penis, refined that, and after a while he could ejaculate almost instantly. In fact, he became so good at this that he could ejaculate before he even had the message processed through his brain that he was about to ejaculate.

Charles and Diane were in love, and they should have lived happily ever after. However, in the presence of certain secrets, sometimes love is not enough. Neither is four minutes of thrusting.

Diane:

I had three men wanting to marry me, and I picked Charles because I thought, of the three, he would be the best lover. I was in love with Charles since I was nineteen and . . . when Charles turned out to be a speed demon, well, my mother told me to wait and see, some of these things solve themselves if you don't overreact. . . . I don't know, now. I wonder if I ever loved him.

Unfortunately, Diane's mother had no idea about the masturbatory tricks of some fourteen-year-old boys or about the series of "hot" dates some men have that get them into the habit of coming fast, or about what her daughter might do to slow down such a man.

The Basic Facts of Premature Ejaculation: Why It Happens; How to Stop It

Few people understand that a man who ejaculates rapidly *causes* himself to do that. It is not that he does such a thing because he is a mean person who wants to make himself and his lover miserable. When he does something to his body that makes that body overreact, he is unaware that his actions have a cause-and-effect relation. The habitual rapid ejaculator—like Charles—rushes his arousal, keeps that arousal speeding along, and (surprise to him) his body orgasms. As far as the man can see, he has done nothing at all. His own actions would be the last place he would look to find the source of his problem. This man, who has just topped his own previous record by ejaculating after only fifteen seconds of arousal, sees himself as a helpless victim of a sexual body gone out of control.

Wrong view.

How a Man Times Ejaculation

Sexual biology is exquisitely simple: erotic arousal, more erotic arousal, ejaculation. All men who come too soon at that moment have the same problem: too much arousal. In fact, all men who *come* are part of that same simple biology. *All men, when they ejaculate, are part of a continuum.* The man who ejaculates in fifteen seconds, the man who ejaculates in two minutes, the man who ejaculates in five minutes, seven minutes, fifteen minutes, are all performing the same biological scenario: the man puts himself in a situation in which he is *so* aroused that he passes the point of ejaculatory inevitability, loses control, and ejaculates.

Biology of the Timing of Ejaculation

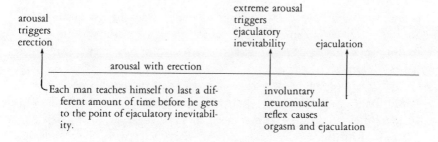

The Moment of Ejaculatory Inevitability

That's the key. There is a point during Charles's arousal when his autonomic nervous system takes over. Once he reaches that point of arousal there is nothing he can do: his body will have a neuromuscular reflex; he will ejaculate. To last longer he has to stretch out the time *before* he reaches the point of ejaculatory inevitability.

Some men, without knowing exactly how they do it, teach themselves to stretch the time to twenty minutes, some to ten minutes, some to only three minutes, and some last only fifteen seconds. So the amount of time a man lasts is up to him. Any man who follows the techniques to lower arousal can teach himself to last longer. He can go from five minutes to fifteen, if that's what he wants, or forty-five seconds to twenty or thirty minutes if that's what he wants.

Unfortunately, most men think the time between getting an erection and coming is natural to their bodies. Like Charles, most men think, This is the way I am. My body is doing this to me.

Or they think the rapid ejaculation is caused by:

- Hormones.
- A vasectomy.
- A wife.
- Gonorrhea.
- Surgery—for anything from prostate to a broken leg.
- An old automobile accident.

Wrong belief.

Ejaculation always occurs because of extreme erotic stimulation.

So we do know what causes a man to come before he wants to. He comes because his arousal is too high. To last longer, he has to lower his arousal. And we do know exactly how he can do that. We know the techniques to lower arousal. Premature ejaculation can be cured in a few hours in 99 percent of cases.

Again, as with typhoid fever, the cure for premature ejaculation was found years ago. And again, like typhoid, premature ejaculation should be an extinct condition. No man need come before he wants to. There is nothing in his body that makes him do that. To control his timing he simply has to learn to lower his arousal.

What is curious is that so many men don't. The number of men who report that premature ejaculation is a disabling condition, which was 25 percent in the 1950s, when the successful American cure was published, is now, some thirty years later, 35 percent.

Charles, like all the others, doesn't know about the techniques and doesn't search for the information, because he believes his "body comes too fast all by itself." It does, but only because *Charles* did something.

Establishing a Biological Pattern

What Charles doesn't realize is that he has altered his natural biology. After so many years of coming fast, he has forgotten his teenage masturbatory tricks. But his body remembers. He has trained his body to react to erotic stimuli at breakneck speed. And that is exactly what his body continues to do.

What he has done is condition his neuromuscular genital reflex, much as he conditioned his other muscles—to run, to dance, to make a series of moves on their own—nearly unconsciously. The man starts the series— the muscles follow through. Like a dancer who learns to waltz—one, two, three, one, two, three—and then, after a few months, hears the first notes of the music: he holds his partner, and without any *conscious* thought on his part, his feet move in the pattern of a waltz. His body goes on automatic.

The lover teaches his muscles much faster than the dancer because he gets a fantastic reward: *orgasm*. Orgasm is an incredibly powerful reinforcer. Rather quickly, a pattern goes into effect, and from then on—the original reason for the pattern is of only historical interest—it is the *pattern* that counts. Men can establish patterns easily by getting too aroused too fast. In addition to establishing a pattern by arousing himself to orgasm when he is alone, many a man establishes a rapid ejaculation pattern when he makes love in one of the five circumstances nearly guaranteed to make a man come too fast.

Making a Man Come Too Fast: Five Causes and Five Hundred Situations

1. *Infrequent orgasms*

This is the most common cause of rapid ejaculation. The man who has *not* had an orgasm for several days will be highly aroused and most likely to lose control.

- He gives up masturbation because he believes it is a childish habit unbecoming to an adult married man. He doesn't have sex for seven days: when he does, he comes immediately.

- His lover is in New York on business. On her return, he rushes to make love to her and almost immediately he ejaculates.

- He is in the hospital having a prostate operation. On his return, he eagerly resumes his sex life, only to find that he almost immediately ejaculates.

- He fights with his wife—the fight and the consequent sexual abstinence last two weeks. The lovers fall into each other's arms to make up, only to experience disappointment when he ejaculates immediately on penetration. She mistakenly interprets his rapid ejaculation as a form of continued hostility.

- He has never had an orgasm with a woman. The first time he has penis-in-the-vagina intercourse, his arousal goes sky high, and he comes immediately. As could be expected. Then, knowing nothing of sexual physiology, he worries that he is stuck with a body that ejaculates too fast.

2. *Prolonged arousal after penetration*

The second most common cause of loss of control. The man who limits his sex life to immediate penetration and continual thrusting can expect to come
—before his wife has an orgasm
—before he is ready to come
—in less than five minutes.

- She insists that he thrust through to orgasm because once they stopped and he lost his erection: she mistakenly believes that stopping may cause impotence. She fears having an impotent husband, so she settles for having a husband who ejaculates prematurely. The truth is that her fear is unfounded. Her husband can last as long as he wants.

- He fears loss of erection, so he rushes to penetrate as soon as he gets an erection, then he rushes to ejaculate as fast as he can before he loses his erection. The irony here is that this method nearly guarantees chronic loss of control, and the rushing makes impotence more likely.

3. *Prolonged arousal before penetration*

- He fondles his sleepy wife: he gets more aroused, she wakes up and wants to begin sexual activity; he's already aroused, penetrates, and comes before he wants to. He's disappointed; she's angry.

182

4. *New sexual variations*

- She appears naked, sits on his lap, and begins to unbutton his shirt; before penetration, he loses control.

- He sees an erotic movie.

- He has long suppressed his desire for oral sex; she mouths his penis for a while, and he loses control.

- She encloses his penis between her breasts, wriggles voluptuously, and he loses control.

- She oils her body and slides over him breathing the words, "I want you. I want you."

- He penetrates from behind, leans over, bites the back of her neck, and comes on the ninth thrust.

5. *New lovers*

The first time with a new lover is most erotic.

- He has been trying to have sex with her for a month, he thinks about her body all day long, he gets an erection the moment he is alone with her. At her place they are playing around in a bubble bath, she runs into the living room, where she lies back on her towel; he penetrates and comes.

Knowing the situations of arousal that are most likely to increase the man's chances of losing control, what are lovers to do?

Immediate action: understand that occasional loss of control is absolutely inconsequential. The danger lies in establishing a pattern. If a man gets into some situation that gets him so excited he loses control, he should avoid getting into a second high-arousal situation—or a third. Once his body gets used to ejaculating quickly after being aroused, his body may just keep on doing that, unless he does something to break the pattern.

Charles—like many men—never considers breaking his pattern. He can't. He doesn't even know he has one.

Charles grows up and lives away from his mother. He has no fear of discovery, his social environment has changed, he no longer has any reason to ejaculate rapidly. But by the time he moves out of his mother's house, he has ejaculated rapidly so many times that his body has established a premature-ejaculation pattern.

On the day he meets the first great love of his life, he faces a crisis. Charles desperately wants to slow down. He wants to get control. For Diane. Now everything has changed, everything *social*. Charles makes fine distinctions between masturbation, which he considers kid stuff, and his desire for an intimate, fulfilling, physical relationship with Diane. But his autonomic nervous system is incapable of such sophisticated thought. Social distinctions are beyond the body's power. The autonomic nervous system is biological. Erection and ejaculation are reflex actions.

Charles can't understand how to change his body. He is unaware—or simply forgetful of—how many times he was pleased to ejaculate rapidly. With his desire for Diane, he expects his body to adjust. It does not. With a new lover, his arousal goes up. This being the very first time he has planned to have an orgasm with any woman, his arousal goes up. Charles is puzzled. This terrible nameless demon that has controlled his body since he was in high school is getting more powerful. He feels helpless.

No need. It's simple for Charles—or any man—to learn to last as long as he wants.

How?

To last as long as he wants, Charles has to learn some basics. First written into medical books by physicians in China before the birth of Christ, the basic plan to delay ejaculation reappeared thirty years ago when North Carolina urologist Dr. James Semans published a new method—very like the Chinese method—by which couples could reverse premature ejaculation in four or five weeks with three hours of his counseling. And twelve years ago, Masters and Johnson published their method—very like the thirty-year-old Semans method, which was very like the two-thousand-year-old Chinese method. Physicians using some variation of the method have replicated these physicians' amazing results, reporting restoration of ejaculatory control in 99 percent of couples.

The simplest thing for Charles to do is copy the people who were the best.

The First Cure for Premature Ejaculation

The man walking through the streets of Peking two thousand years ago had the same basic penis, testicles, and autonomic nervous system as the man walking through the streets of Washington, D.C., today. The difference: The man in ancient China was *motivated* to make love for hours without ejaculating.

Control was the issue. Records of the rites of the Chou Dynasty tell us that the Chinese man, like his emperor—whose sex patterns he duplicated with fewer lovers—had sex by the numbers. First, numbers of women. Every month the emperor had sex with one hundred twenty-one women, representing the nearest round number to one-third of the three hundred sixty-five days of the year. His strenuous duty was to bring all his one hundred eight concubines to orgasm in groups of nine on consecutive nights without ejaculating himself. Every time he performed this feat he absorbed Yin from the female ejaculate which, in turn, strengthened his Yang which helped him with his goal of impregnating (with a male child) his nine spouses, three consorts, and, most important, the empress. He brought these women to orgasm by a short period of thrusts delivered in sets of nine—and then he let himself go—at the exact conceptual hour determined by the court astrologer. The Chinese man's sex life—like his emperor's—was a numerological masterpiece.

Numbers were important. Records were kept. Ejaculation was withheld.

This great control gave the man power. Not only could he make love to many women in the same night, he could do something even more important: he could be assured when he did finally ejaculate he would have a son.

They further believed that by withholding his ejaculation a man could prevent his own death. The withheld sperm, or so they imagined, traveled from the testicles up the spinal column, into the brain, where the sperm revitalized the brain marrow, allowing the man to go on living.

These were the beliefs of an ancient people who dealt every day with a

185

universe they found mysterious, powerful, and out of their control. By controlling their sex lives they felt they could synchronize with nature and, by that action, put a stop to the chaotic universe.

Rapid ejaculation was absolutely forbidden. How could a Chinese man allow himself to come too fast, believing as he did that, by losing control, he was ejaculating away not only his own life but the lives of his unborn sons, and that he might even be acting to bring a rapid end to the world.

So they did teach themselves timing control. They were the most proficient group ever at doing that.

How did they do it?

They acted to lower their arousal. Though they may have had no idea of the basis of the science of arousal, they did follow the right biological rules.

The Four Secrets That Help a Man Last as Long as He Wants

Become a master of foreplay. Faced with up to nine women a night, the Chinese man *had* to give up dependence on thrusting. Thrusting is the way a man usually receives the most extreme arousal; if you don't want to receive the most extreme arousal, don't thrust. Needless to say, thrusting was a minor part of the last-forever Chinese sex life. It had to be. Anyway, the man's orgasm was not the goal; the goal was the woman's orgasm. Therefore, penis-in-the-vagina intercourse, man-on-top, thrust-and-come was not the goal. Lovemaking was geared to give the man the greatest opportunity to withhold his orgasm. Chinese erotic art shows that cunnilingus was highly advocated. Sucking of breasts was favored. The man who was desperate to bring a woman to orgasm with the fewest strokes—done, of course, in sets of nine—was a man who was a master of the hand and the tongue.

Make love to an easily orgasmic woman. The woman who claimed sexual innocence, who said she knew nothing about how she might have an orgasm and wouldn't tell if she did, was a dangerous woman. From an early age women were encouraged to masturbate. They became highly skilled in the knowledge of their arousal system. It was a rare woman who failed to orgasm. The Chinese man, who had to keep his erection through fe-

186

male orgasm after female orgasm, was a man who truly appreciated a sexually knowledgeable woman.

Practice stopping and starting over. A man who expects to make love for hours has to rest. Besides, increasing unbroken arousal builds from low to high, always leading to ejaculation. Always. If you do *not* want to ejaculate, you have to stop before the point of ejaculatory inevitability. If you do not stop, you will come. The Chinese lovers would stop, the man's arousal would go down, they would start over.

Ejaculate frequently. If you had been there at the time to talk to one of these fellows, he would have denied that he ejaculated. However, he did. Ancient records describe his habit of practicing *huan ching* (known in the West as *coitus Saxonius*): by pressing the urethra between the scrotum and anus (the *p'ing-i* point) he prevented the sperm from passing out of the penis. The sperm—as he ejaculated—went, as it must, into the bladder. The ancient Chinese man reports that he did this quite often as he happily, but mistakenly, believed that by doing this he was sending his sperm up his spine to his brain, where the sperm would work its magical powers of rejuvenation. No matter what he believed he was doing, he was having orgasms rather frequently. Any man who ejaculates frequently will slow down. Frequent ejaculation causes the body to react more slowly to erotic stimuli. The man who has a number of orgasms a week will take longer to become aroused and longer still to become highly aroused enough to ejaculate.

Okay. Those are the basics.

1. Become a master of foreplay.
2. Make love to an easily orgasmic woman.
3. Practice stopping . . . and starting over.
4. Ejaculate frequently.

The Revised Cure

American physicians have refined the system. Their instructions to lower arousal till control is established are more precise. Still, the advice is the same.

Dr. Annon's Method

The simplest therapy is the one advocated by sex therapist Jack Annon. He tells his patients to do one thing. Follow Rule 4: Ejaculate frequently. Rearousal after orgasm takes longer. Biological fact. So he advises men to double their standard number of weekly orgasms. If that fails to stop their rapid ejaculation, he has them double the number of orgasms again. Dr. Annon reports this solves the problem for most of his patients.

Dr. Semans's Method

The method most used by sex therapists is Dr. James Semans's thirty-year-old stop-start system. Rather than organizing an entire society to have sex in the ways that make it easiest for the man to control his timing, Dr. Semans organizes the two lovers to follow the four rules.

Rule 1: *Become a master of foreplay.* You and your lover are to practice erotic caressing of each other's genitals with your hands. Your wife is to stimulate your penis with her hands. At the same time you are to caress her genitals.

Rule 2: *Make love to an easily orgasmic woman.* Help her to become one by separating her orgasm from your thrusting. Temporarily, during the therapy, you are to be sure she is caressed to orgasm, whether or not you come rapidly.

Rule 3: *Practice stopping . . . and starting over.*

With a dry penis: As your arousal builds, you remove her hand from your penis—*before* the point of ejaculatory inevitability. Practice stopping, letting your arousal go down, and starting over. Stop four times: on the fifth time you caress each other to orgasm. If you guess wrong and come accidentally, caress your lover to orgasm. This way each lover learns more about the erotic pacing of the other. Control and building to orgasm together becomes easier for the two of you. When you and your lover can pace yourselves so your dry erect penis stays erect without ejaculation as long as you wish, add a lubricant.

With a slippery penis: As your arousal builds you develop tolerance for the highly arousing slippery feel of the inside of her vagina. Practice stopping and starting in the same way, stretching out the time before

188

ejaculation, until your slippery erect penis can tolerate erotic caress as long as you wish. When this happens, add penis-in-the-vagina intercourse.

Rule 4: *Ejaculate frequently.* The Semans stop-start practice sessions always end in ejaculation. Naturally, as the number of practice sessions increases, so does the number of ejaculations.

Results: With eight cases of lovers who had suffered from rapid ejaculation over periods of two months to fifteen years, all lovers reported an end to the problem after practicing four to five weeks.

The Masters and Johnson Additions

While the stop-start system is the basic method, some sex therapists add variations to increase the couple's control. For instance, Masters and Johnson suggest that after the husband signals his wife to stop caressing his penis, *she is to squeeze his penis, front and back, just below the head.* After he loses his erection, she is to begin the caress again.

They further add to the stop-start system by extending the number of practice sessions to include penis-in-the-vagina intercourse. *Stop-start with quiet containment:* Positioning herself on top of you, your lover inserts your erect penis in her vagina. She does not move. You do *not* thrust. At your signal, before your arousal reaches the point of ejaculatory inevitability, she lifts off and squeezes your penis just below the head. When you lose your erection she starts to caress your penis again. You repeat the five stop-start trials with your lover lifting off and squeezing at consecutive sessions until you can last indefinitely. *Then you repeat the stop-start with gentle thrusting controlled by the woman.* While gently thrusting in the same position you stop and start with your lover lifting off and squeezing until you can last indefinitely.

Results: Masters and Johnson report that after three days' practice stopping and starting with the squeeze technique, ability to tolerate stimulation of the penis usually increased to fifteen to twenty minutes. By the end of the two weeks at the Masters and Johnson Foundation, 98 percent of their couples (182 of 186) were able to maintain thrusting long enough for the wife to orgasm in half the attempts at penis-in-the-vagina intercourse.

Every technique works because every technique lowers arousal. To solve your problem, start with the easiest technique and add to it as you discover you need more. If doubling the number of your ejaculations gives you the control you want, fine, stop. If you find stopping and starting with hand caress gives you control, great, stop there. If you feel you need to add the squeeze technique—and continue to practice stopping and starting during intercourse—do that. One technique is not necessarily better than another—they are simply different ways of doing the same thing: lowering arousal. That's all Charles has to do. As soon as he practices being erotic *while* lowering his arousal, he cures himself of premature ejaculation.

Question: If this information has been around so long, why hasn't Charles used it? Because Charles is a man of his culture. He has been taught to keep quiet about erotic sex. And to believe that *everything* sexual—even the way he masturbates—is a natural phenomenon. And also to believe that there is nothing about sex he doesn't already know. In fact, as a teenager he took some pride in being far ahead of the other boys—he was the only fourteen-year-old he knew who could come in less than sixty seconds.

This fact confuses Charles; he mistakenly feels that—*naturally*—he is in some ways such a sexual powerhouse that he is really all right. He expects that any day now his body will stop doing this to him. And he has yet to unravel his confusion by facing the three truths about premature ejaculation.

Truth #1 About Premature Ejaculation
The man who ejaculates prematurely is a biological success.

The man who loses his erection has failed biologically. However, the man who loses control and has an orgasm has *not* failed—he is only doing what every normal person is supposed to do: lose control and have an orgasm. He is a biological success. It is only the *timing* of his success that is out of control, which makes no difference at all when he masturbates, or when he pets, or when he is with a woman who wants him to come fast. It becomes a problem only when he wants to bring a woman to orgasm by slow and repeated thrusting. Then uncontrolled ejaculation is an enormous problem.

Truth #2 About Premature Ejaculation
The man who ejaculates prematurely for more than a month will continue in that pattern unless he does something to lower his arousal prior to ejaculation.

Charles read in a sex book that a true premature ejaculator either ejaculates in less than thirty seconds after penetrating or is unable to bring his wife to orgasm 50 percent of the time. He says to himself he may not be a real premature ejaculator because he lasts longer than thirty seconds. Moreover, he feels that it's absurd to use the reactions of a woman's body to measure whether or not a man's body is working right. He's correct on both counts, but no matter. For Charles's peace of mind—and every man's—this is the truth.

Truth #3 About Premature Ejaculation
At any time when a man ejaculates before he wants to he is ejaculating prematurely.

And, since any man can learn to last as long as he and his lover want, there's no need to come too fast. The cure works. Charles, like all lovers, can pace his arousal.
So what's the problem?
Lovers.

How He Fails to Succeed

Lovers are highly emotional creatures. With many techniques to lower arousal readily available, they are likely to rush off in the wrong direction, trying every second to do the only thing they've been taught to do—get higher, higher, higher, and come.
Wrong choice for a rapid ejaculator.
But that was all Charles could think of, and at age twenty, he lost all chance of regaining control because he fell in love with Diane, who was—

Choosing the Worst Kind of Lover

Diane quite innocently did to Charles what she would do to any sexually overreactive man—she caused havoc with his biology. Charles desperately needs to develop techniques to force his arousal *down*. With Diane he didn't have a chance. Every single thing they did together sent his arousal up, up, up.

Charles's body doesn't recognize his charming wife's cherubic good looks, her intense love, or her good intentions. Unfortunately, Charles's autonomic nervous system is dumb. His body registers only Charles's response to each of her actions. Is this erotic action too arousing? That's all.

Judged solely on how her actions affect Charles's susceptibility to ejaculating rapidly, Diane is a disaster.

First of all, *she refuses to let Charles become a master of foreplay.* Diane tells Charles she does not want him touching her "down there." She had never touched her genitals and when Charles tried, she said, "I don't believe that's *necessary* for you to *touch* me *there*. I don't like it. It makes me feel uncomfortable. Besides, now that we're married we can do the real thing."

Diane limits their sex life to one major action—penis-in-the-vagina and thrust. Which immediately puts Charles in the highest arousal situation. Diane insists. She even tells herself that this *is* what Charles wants too.

Impasse.

Then, *she refuses to become easily orgasmic.* Diane knows nothing about how to have an orgasm and is proud of it. While Charles was busy connecting his body to every possible erotic stimulus, Diane was waiting for a man to awaken her. Charles tried. He tried to touch her clitoris. He even tried straight talk, telling her that many women had orgasms *only* after clitoral caress. Diane disagreed: "I am going to have vaginal orgasms. I know it." Diane pins her hopes for an orgasm on Charles's being able to thrust long enough—no matter how long it takes. And so, at her insistence, every sexual experience turns into a performance test for Charles.

And she refuses to let him stop and start over. Any time Charles stops to rest, Diane becomes livid.

I feel rejected. I feel . . . somehow it isn't right. It makes me angry. I'm getting excited and he stops. I won't let him get away with that. All I know—I want him to put his penis in my vagina and I don't want him to take it out.

And so, by her own decisions, innocent Diane raises her husband's arousal level threefold. Then, the erotic body being a biological organism, biology takes its course. Charles ejaculates rapidly. More and more often. He is deeply embarrassed. Charles feels so bad, he can't look at his wife. Confronted with a lover who frequently sprays his sperm on her belly, the romantic lady is in shock.

I can't imagine why he does that, but it is making me absolutely furious. If he doesn't stop that, it'll be a long time before he can expect me to make love to him.

Next, Diane does what many women do in her situation—*she makes sure he ejaculates less frequently.* Diane withdraws from sex. She tells herself this will be good for Charles. This way he'll have all the pressure off. Innocently—and with the best intentions—she once again interferes with his ability to control his ejaculation. By withdrawing from him sexually, she increases her attractiveness to him, and, with no orgasm, the man who needs to lower his arousal finds that his arousal goes up. His ejaculation comes faster.

What Charles needs is a woman who knows how to help a man lower his arousal. Diane is not the woman. She is adamant that everything is Charles's responsibility and Charles's fault. Diane takes no responsibility for what they do together in bed. Premature ejaculation, that is his problem. Her failure to orgasm. That is also his problem.

These two problems—premature ejaculation and female failure to orgasm—are often found together. She stays unaware of how high her arousal needs to go because she never gets high enough arousal from his penis. He never has a chance to slow his arousal down because of her penis-in-the-vagina demands. A deadly team: both lovers help each other lose.

But in this case only one of them feels the responsibility to do something: Charles. Convinced that everything would be fine if Charles could only learn to thrust longer, Diane demands that he try. And he does try.

He Tries to Cure Himself: The Five Worst Mistakes a Man Can Make

Okay, what Charles—and all men—have to do is *decrease* their sensitivity. Charles tried. Ironically every single thing Charles tried to do to *decrease* his arousal did the opposite: it *increased* his arousal.

His first mistake really couldn't be helped. He met Diane.

1. *Charles stays close to a woman.* For Charles, who could come in less than a minute by stimulating his penis and looking at a shiny colored picture of a naked woman, being close to a real live woman sends his arousal up, up, up.

2. *Charles worries.* He is extremely anxious about performing sexually. For some men, performance anxiety slows them down—so much, in fact, that they fail to get enough arousal to trigger an erection. We know that men and women can become so sexually anxious that their anxiety can block all sexual reflexes: erection, lubrication, or orgasm. Charles's reaction is the opposite. Anxiety makes his arousal go up and his ejaculation come faster. Sexual arousal is made up of direct sexual arousal *plus general arousal.* Charles's anxiety heightens his general arousal. Charles is already supersensitive to sexual stimuli; now he is more generally aroused to the things around him—like Diane, and the idea of what might happen while they make love, which in turn sends his arousal up again.

3. *Charles tries to stop thinking about sex.* He is determined to "hold on" until the last minute. Much of the time he's making love he's reciting ball scores, thinking of garbage, going over his multiplication tables. It seems logical, but doesn't work. The reason: When Charles finally does think about sex, his anxiety over whether or not he is going to ejaculate rapidly causes him to push, which sends his arousal up again.

4. *Charles tries sex with a new lover.* It's difficult for anyone to admit to a sexual problem, and everyone has an easy escape hatch: "Maybe it's not me, maybe it's my lover's fault." Charles has a wonderful rationalization for hopping into bed with Lisa. "Maybe with Lisa, I'll last a

long time, and then I'll have more confidence, and then this will help me last longer with my wife." And, in an effort to give him and Lisa the best chance to make love with no expectations of difficulty, he doesn't tell Lisa about his problem. Of course, being terribly anxious with a new live woman, only one thing can happen. His arousal goes sky high. He ejaculates on penetration.

5. *Charles gives up orgasms.* That was not his plan. He planned to lower his arousal drastically by giving up masturbation. First he thought, Now that I have a wife, I am embarrassed to be doing this "kid stuff." Charles, who had been masturbating two or three times a day, was tired of doing that—and resented the fact that he had to. Besides after a while it didn't seem to work so well. (It wouldn't *because* he simultaneously raised his arousal.) And he was afraid that in the long run it was bad for him. It seemed to him that he was just putting in more practice at premature ejaculation.

So he stopped masturbation. Boomerang. Unfortunately, as he gave up masturbation, he also gave up having orgasms.

And then, every time he attempted penis-in-the-vagina intercourse, he did what he was fated to do, he came fast. Faster. Faster. Faster.

Having only another failure to look forward to, and another encounter with an angry wife, Charles then did—what most chronic premature ejaculators do—the worst possible thing: he avoided sex. He met his wife's withdrawal with a withdrawal of his own.

Charles was soon caught in a circle of failure.

The Circle of Failure

Premature Ejaculation: The Circle of Failure

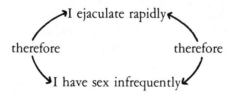

195

Charles was a man in a desperate circumstance. He had to lower his arousal. In five years of marriage that never happened. She raised his arousal. He raised his arousal. Until all they had left were the worries, the rationalizations, bitter words, and finally the divorce.

Charles:

Would you believe I love Diane. I always have. I guess I still do. She is sexy. But she's difficult. I loved her being so sexually ... well, quiet ... at first ... now I can't stand it. I can't give her what she wants. There is no way on heaven's earth I can thrust till that woman comes.

I'm afraid to say anything. We never talk. The problem is there. But neither of us mentions it. Oh ... would you believe ... I got so furious ... we had this fight ... she said I was just out for myself ... and I screamed that she was frigid. I really wanted to throw something at her ... and I never apologized. Anyway, if I said something to her, what would I say? Whatever I said, she'd take it the wrong way. There are some women you can talk to about sex and some you can't. Diane you can't talk to.

It could be her fault. You know, I'm certain ... well, almost certain that I was lasting at least four minutes ... right after we got married. Now ... I don't know ... I come right away ... fifteen seconds ... would you believe ... we have sex ... say, once every couple of months ... *when* I can get an erection. Would you believe, most of the time now I can't even get it up. I've ... it's probably something to do with my hormones. I'm afraid to have sex with her. I'm worried ... she's going to get too impatient if I don't perform. Sometimes ... would you believe ... I wish I could be with a more accepting woman.

Diane:

I do know that I feel that if he really loved me, he would last longer. This coming so fast, you know ... it's a way of being hostile to women. I read that. I've been reading quite a bit. Something also about hatred of the father. And I read an article that shows this woman living with a speed demon and she says she doesn't care. She focuses on his *attentiveness*. Probably all made up anyway. I also read a sex book for women. The therapist advised women in

196

my shoes to "do other things." But I don't want to spend my whole life like that ... I want to have an orgasm before I die. Well ... I've been thinking I may have to have it with somebody else.

I used to worry that maybe I wasn't sexy enough ... or maybe I had a bad smell ... I don't know. Well, I do know ... it's his problem. But it's my sex life. What have I got? A speed demon who comes in ten seconds. He only wants to have sex once a month. I have been so angry for so ... it's very unlike me ... but finally I just told him ... I won't take your shit. You are only interested in your own orgasm, you are hostile, you are hopeless as a lover, you have ruined my life ... and ...

He leaves her.

The First Step to Success: Rejecting Her Rejection

The toughest speech of Charles's life, this one took him five years to make. Feeling that his premature ejaculation was *his* problem, Charles had always felt grateful she stayed with him. He accepted her continued rejection. When he finally figured out that he had a human right to be with an accepting lover, a loving lover, he rejected her rejection.

We could be close, we could work around my problem, we could go for help, we could do something to stay close sexually, but you have some problem that keeps us from doing anything to get closer. I'd like to help you, but you won't let me. I need a warm sexual relationship. I miss being in love. Goodbye.

An important act. Charles was free.

At first being free was not so great. There he was, divorced, impotent half the time, ejaculating too rapidly the rest of the time, and terrified of being alone with a woman. Then he met Susan. And, of course, the worst happened.

He came. At her house. After only a couple of kisses and one lick of her nipple. Which startled her. Charles, embarrassed to death, describes that first time naked with Susan looking at his sperm on the wallpaper as the worst moment of his life. Full of apologies he said, "If you don't want to go out with me again, I'll understand. I'm sorry. I'm really sorry."

Her words were a surprise:
>Sorry for what? That I'm so sexy I drive you wild? That you make me feel good? That I like you?

The confident Susan took the situation in stride. "Wait a second," she says, "I'll bring you a robe."

Charles:
>At least she didn't run to the bathroom and cry like Diane.

Running and crying is not for Susan. She is sexually secure. Although, like all of us, she is vulnerable, still she looks forward to lovemaking. She is used to having orgasms, and she knows that her body works fine. She has what one might call sexual integrity. She knows her body, her emotions, and how they operate. And she knows that each man has a sexuality separate from hers, that each man has his own sexual history, his own unique body, and that much of what he does has nothing to do with her—and everything to do with him. Susan knows the boundaries between her sexuality and his sexuality. Among the things she tells him as they talk through the night:

- I don't want to shock you, but I'm thirty years old and I have seen sperm before.
- You may think of yourself as a sex object, but I don't. I'm here because you attract me, you have a sweetness and a kindness I like to be near.
- Some doctors are very sophisticated about sex problems now. You might want to find a physician who specializes in treating rapid ejaculation.
- I'm sorry this makes you feel so bad, I don't like to see you so unhappy—but please don't feel bad on my account. I am not

upset or bothered or anything. I only feel . . . I feel like helping you.

And that's how Susan became Charles's second wife.

During their first eighteen months together, Charles's second wife did everything right—to lower his arousal.

- She made sure she got excited enough during foreplay so she could come with limited thrusting.
- Sometimes she separated her orgasms from his thrusting entirely, lying close to him while he touched her clitoris and vagina.
- She was happy stopping and starting, using different positions, having oral sex, making love with no expectation that he would even put his penis in her vagina.
- And, because she was so accepting and happily close to her husband in those three ways, they had sex three, four, five times a week. Which increased the number of Charles's orgasms—and *decreased* the number of times he came too fast.

They could have continued with these healthy patterns, but Charles was discontented. Charles wanted more control. True, the impotence vanished when he no longer felt the pressure to thrust longer than he could. And he did last longer—one minute, two minutes. Once or twice, three minutes. But there was no consistency. Fifteen seconds was still a real possibility, though no longer a cause of fear, humiliation, or marital hysteria. Sympathetic to Charles's wish for more control, Susan was supportive and sensitive.

They went to a therapist who helped them progress through the stop-start system.

He and His Best Lover Follow the Stop-Start System

1. Temporarily discontinue penis-in-the-vagina intercourse.
2. Sexual contact limited to the low-arousal situation of hand caress of erect, dry penis. Caress to increase arousal four times. Stop each time *before* ejaculatory inevitability. Squeeze the penis

below the head. The erection will subside. Start again. On the fifth time caress to orgasm.

3. Caress wife's genitals to climax.

4. When you can last as long as you want, proceed through a series of higher-arousal situations—stop-start with hand caress of lubricated penis, stop-start with quiet vaginal containment, stop-start with gentle thrusting.

Questions About the System:

She: But won't I hurt him?

A: You cannot hurt an erect penis by squeezing. You do want to lower his arousal. The squeeze should be uncomfortable enough that he loses his erection.

She: Where do I put my fingers?

A: Below the head of the penis. Use your thumb and forefinger, squeezing front to back. Squeeze for five seconds.

She: Do I have to be on top?

A: Yes. This is the position that gives the man greatest control of his timing. It also is the position in which it is easiest for you to stop and squeeze.

He: What if I want to ejaculate?

A: Don't. Until you have practiced stopping and starting four times. After you ejaculate, you will lose your desire. You will be unable to get an erection and, therefore, unable to build an extended time before ejaculation.

He: How long will it take for me to gain control?

A: Your body is unique. Your needs are unique. Practice until you can control the length of time. When you have extended the length of time before ejaculation so that it is as long as you want, stop.

He: How long can I stay erect without ejaculating?

A: Everyone is different. In theory, a man can extend his latency to ejaculation for hours. He can certainly last beyond the time when it would be of any use to do so.

If the system works so well, why do Charles and Susan need supervision? Because Charles—being such a long-term self-trained rapid ejaculator—will be reluctant to give up this habit. So will his body. In his case, all the things that could possibly go wrong just might.

The Pitfalls of Learning to Last

He Comes Too Quickly

Session 1: It's to be expected, if you have always come too quickly—even with the system—that the first thing you'll do is come too quickly. That's the seemingly impossible dilemma: How is Charles—whose problem is his inability to stop *before* the moment of ejaculatory inevitability—going to know how to do that so he can carry out the system? The answer: He won't—for a while.

Susan caresses his penis against the outside of her vagina. Before any signal even gets to his brain that would tell him he is aroused he comes.

Even with the support of the system, which gives Charles less to do, which puts Susan equally in charge, so that Charles can focus on recognizing how to stop *before* the moment of ejaculatory inevitability, Charles struggles to guess when to stop. Charles guesses wrong. That's to be expected. Charles and Susan wait a few hours or a day and try again.

The next time, he comes on the third stop-squeeze. That night he comes on the first stop-squeeze. The next morning he successfully stops three times in a row—and he is afraid to try again. *He decides it is better to quit while he is successful.*

Wrong decision.

He should continue through the fourth and fifth trial. While he practices extending his latency, he will guess wrong. That's okay. When he does, he is to wait a while and practice again. The wrong guesses are unimportant. They become important only if Charles pays attention to them and stops practicing. With practice, he will guess right more often.

For the truly frustrated, there is always the clock. If your usual time is thirty seconds, *do not guess,* go by the clock. First trial, squeeze at fifteen seconds. Wait. Second trial, squeeze at twenty-five seconds. Wait. Third trial, squeeze at forty seconds. Wait. Fourth trial, squeeze at forty-five seconds. Fifth trial, caress to orgasm. The crucial step: Be sure to hold off ejaculation a bit *longer* at each trial.

Unrealized Expectations

Session 5: Charles and Susan are disappointed. His longest timing to ejaculation has been three minutes.

Charles:
>Three minutes is *not* a long time. And, anyway, I'm tired of this "couples masturbation" nonsense. It is a ridiculous thing for a married couple to do. We gave it a good try.

Charles says this in the resigned voice of a man ready to quit. But Susan is ready for her husband's frustration.

Susan:
>Don't think about whether it's working or not working or how well it's working. That's the same worry story I've heard from you since the first day we met. Let go of judging yourself. The doctor says it works. The doctor says to do it. Just do it.

Susan is right. The system has a cumulative effect. Quite often couples practice for five or six sessions: no change. And then the man's control changes dramatically. In Charles's case, he stays on the one-to-three-minute plateau through six sessions—then goes to eight minutes, ten and a half minutes, fifteen minutes. Which Charles and Susan decide is long enough.

They go to a situation of higher arousal: caress of the lubricated penis.

The Sequential-Thinking Handicap

Session 9: Feeling Susan's hands sliding over his slippery penis, Charles becomes highly aroused. He guesses right but has to signal her to squeeze at forty-five seconds. The next day he lasts four minutes, but in the following session he has to signal Susan to squeeze first at fifteen seconds, then ten seconds, then three minutes, and on the fifth trial he comes after only fifteen seconds. He is distraught. I'm a failure, is all he thinks. He tells himself, "I have this problem of coming too fast, I *have always* had this problem, and I will always have this problem. This is the way I am."

Wrong thinking.

Biologically the man's latency-to-ejaculation time does *not* improve steadily or sequentially. *The variability is always there.* Some short trials are to be expected. Charles wants to see steady, continuous improvement. He is taught to think, Now I can do three pushups, now I can do twenty-four pushups. Now, any time I try I can do twenty-four pushups. Though gaining timing control of one's ejaculation does not work that way, Charles expects it to. He is proud to have reached fifteen minutes— panicked to once again experience fifteen seconds. But that is normal. Variability is always present. Some short trials occur. As it is with all men, the short arousal to ejaculation is always present. The goal for a man who habitually comes too quickly is to *decrease* the number of times rapid ejaculation occurs until that number is *so* small that it no longer presents a problem.

How She Helps Him

Session 12: Charles has a marvelous secret weapon: Susan. Susan says, "Yes, I see you are anxious. I'm sorry. But your anxiety is to be expected. I can stand it. Charles, we are going to continue." Susan is a rock. Which is one reason Charles continues to follow the directions, and by Session 12 is lasting fifteen minutes, even though in his entire life he has never expected to last more than four minutes.

Susan is never embarrassed to have an orgasm. At each session's end she has one as her husband caresses her. She ends the session curled in his arms, kissing his neck. Her orgasm is an essential part of breaking his pattern.

Charles's first wife, if she were in Susan's place, would certainly have interfered with the system. Diane might well have spoken the words of many nonorgasmic wives of rapid ejaculators, "I don't like you just grabbing me down there. It feels too rough. It's too confusing. Too much going on; I don't really need this. It makes me feel uncomfortable." Then, getting her way, falling asleep with her back to him, unsatisfied, having added no knowledge about her own arousal system, irritated that sex was still all for *his* orgasm, grudgingly doing her wifely duty, she could reenact the familiar old sex patterns that were driving them apart. Faced with this kind of balky lover, Charles would have to be a determined fellow indeed to change. More likely, on his own, without a therapist, he would let his nonorgasmic wife convince him to forget her orgasm.

Wrong decision.

The Chinese man always brought his lovers to orgasm, thrusting or no thrusting. The successful Dr. Semans insisted that every man he treated bring his wife to orgasm. Why? Because he knew that, in most cases, the wife of a man suffering from rapid ejaculation would be accustomed to getting too little stimulation. He also knew she was used to not asking for it. And he knew that a woman who benefited, from the first session, would be *very* supportive of her husband's continuing the treatment until he was cured.

The wife who says, "That's okay, I don't really want an orgasm. I'm telling you, touching me down there is *unnecessary*. Let's just do the part that helps you," is leading her lover down the garden path.

Two Crises at the Very Last Moment

His Penis Stops Working

Session 15: Poor Charles. Breaking his pattern of quick, high arousal and rapid ejaculation, which he practiced for so many years, is excruciatingly hard. Every time he thinks he's got it, he finds out he hasn't.

During Session 15 the worst happens. Susan squeezes. They wait. She caresses his slick penis against the outside of her vagina. Nothing happens. No erection. Half an hour later, she caresses, stops, squeezes. They wait. She caresses. No erection. Two hours later, she caresses his penis, but he gets only a partial erection.

It's plain to Charles that his body is in worse shape than ever. He is furious. He does everything right. Exactly right. And look what happens. He's becoming impotent.

Charles is terribly upset. At this rate, he says, he'll be spending five hours a day—five *frustrating* hours—doing some silly thing that plainly doesn't work. It might work for other people, but it is apparent that it does not work for him. "I probably have," he says, "some bodily problem that doctors don't know about yet." Charles wants to quit. He believes he will never succeed, faced with the hopeless complexity of a body that doesn't work.

Wrong belief.

Simple explanation. Charles is following the ancient Chinese practice of sending his ejaculate into his bladder. And, like the Chinese man, he doesn't know he is doing that. This is not proof of impending impotence, proof that the treatment doesn't work, or proof that his body doesn't work. The truth is far simpler. Charles still guesses wrong. He told his wife to squeeze—*after the moment of ejaculatory inevitability*. A practiced hand, she squeezed *before* his ejaculate could enter the urethra. Neither lover *saw* any ejaculate. So all that followed looked like a system failure. Rather than being impotent, Charles was performing the quite reputable feat of having three orgasms and regaining his erections three times.

For the next two sessions he cautiously directs Susan to squeeze a bit earlier than would be his natural inclination and once again the system works.

He Succumbs to Lust

Session 18: By this session, Charles is feeling confident he can last indefinitely most of the time and they proceed to a situation of even higher arousal: Charles is to put his erect penis in his lover's quiet vagina and hold still.

Charles is feeling *very* sexy. Seeing those long-lasting erections makes him feel powerful. He is impatient. He *wants* to have intercourse with his wife. He does penetrate her vagina. He is supposed to build his tolerance for quiet containment. Instead, with Susan on top—before she can lift off and squeeze—he thrusts for eight minutes, she comes, he comes, they are happy. They believe he is cured. The next day Charles penetrates—and immediately ejaculates. He feels wretched.

Question: Why does this happen?

Answer: Because Charles got confused. He has learned to get a lasting erection, but that is *not* the goal. The goal is to gain *timing control.*

By having intercourse before he learned timing control, Charles proceeded too rapidly. Because of penetration, his general anxiety and excitement tripled, his arousal went up, and he did what he had to do under the circumstances: he lost control.

True, some men have no need to stop and start with quiet vaginal containment. Some men gain control by simply stopping and starting. Some men need the help of the squeeze with subsequent erection loss. And Charles? Charles needs all the steps. His pattern is too well established. His anxiety is too high. And he is simply too overreactive to erotic stimuli.

Susan and Charles backtrack. After they build his tolerance for quiet containment, they proceed to a situation of extremely high arousal: Charles is to penetrate and gently thrust.

And He Lasts and Lasts and Lasts

Session 22: Straddling her husband, Susan caresses his penis to erection, puts his penis in her vagina. In this relaxed position, Charles thrusts gently till he feels as though he is going to ejaculate. At that point—six minutes—he tells his wife to stop. She lifts herself off, squeezes his erect penis below the head for five seconds, and waits till his erection subsides. She caresses his penis again, then inserts his penis, he thrusts for seven minutes and tells her to stop. She lifts herself off, squeezes, waits for his erection to subside. She starts the sequence again. He helps her coordinate her orgasm to his by stimulating her clitoris as he thrusts. The first night, Charles and his wife orgasm on the fifth trial after twelve minutes of thrusting.

Once again, the lovers have *increased* his arousal. Once again, there is the expected *temporary* shortening of his latency. The latency that had been extended to fifteen minutes with caress of the lubricated penis is now back to twelve minutes.

The next few sessions are easy, because Charles has control. He can stop and start. He can last. Susan has grown accustomed to his body rhythms. He can last indefinitely.

Susan is very happy for her lover. But she is no fool. She knows her man is overreactive. When she met him, sexual intercourse was much too erotic an activity for him. His body *is* highly susceptible to erotic arousal. He will always have that same body. And he could redevelop the same pattern.

Prediction: Should this happen, he is likely to panic: "Oh, Lord, a relapse. Why didn't the doctor *say* it wouldn't last." But the clever second wife will be ready—and, like her spiritual ancestor the great-great-great-great-great Chinese grandmother, she will see that her overreactive lover:

· Becomes a master of foreplay.
· Makes love to an easily orgasmic woman.
· Stops and starts over.
· Ejaculates frequently.

For Susan, premature ejaculation is an extinct condition; she has made it so. Lucky Charles. Lovers.

Ten Laws for Lifetime Success

1. If you've found the perfect way to make love once—find another perfect way. And another. And another. Know that your lover has a new body with all new desire left undiscovered and therefore unsatisfied. And you must rediscover each other's eroticism forever.

2. Teach your lover how to touch you in the unique ways that you want.

3. Give your lover the exact touch your lover—and only your lover—wants.

4. Do things in the right order. Build your desire and let the erections *follow*. Build your desire and let the orgasms follow. All by themselves.

5. Add the erotic delights that will please your lover. The clothing. The sounds. The smells. The tastes. Give each other choices. Give each other new choices.

6. Think of your lover. Think of your lover naked. Think of every way you want to touch your lover. Where. When. Let your thoughts go. Let your thoughts give you pleasure.

7. Take care of your lover's erotic wants completely—sometimes.

8. Let your lover take care of you completely—sometimes.

9. Make love without an erection—sometimes. Make love without climaxing—sometimes.

10. Build a list of the exact things your lover desires. Give each other what you want. Make a new list. Give each other what you want again.

All lovers should practice the laws of sexual success. And keep practicing them forever. The laws that help lovers feel erotic ecstasy should never be a secret.

The real secrets, the important ones, are the secrets that you and your lover have had in your thoughts and in your bodies from the beginning. Those erotic wishes should be secret. They are the love secrets that are just for the two of you to discover—and discover again—lover to lover.

Bibliography

In addition to the couple interviews and the consultations on sex therapy techniques with Gene G. Abel, M.D., the following sources were used:

Abel, Gene G. "The Evolution of Sexual Fantasies." Paper read at 3rd Annual Conference of the Association of Sex Therapists and Counselors in March 1978 in Atlanta, Georgia.

Abel, Gene G., Judith V. Becker, Jerry Cunningham-Rather, Mary Mittelman, and Marshall Primack. "Differential Diagnosis of Impotence in Diabetics: the Validity of Sexual Symptomatology." *Journal of Neurology and Urodynamics* 1: 1982.

Abel Gene G., Judith V. Becker, Jerry Cunningham-Rather, and Mary Mittelman. "Sex Therapy Treatment for Diabetics with Organic Impotence." Paper read at the 1st International Symposium on Impotence and Diabetes Mellitus. Panum Institute, University of Copenhagen, Denmark. August 1982.

Abel, Gene G., and Edward B. Blanchard. "Identifying Specific Erotic Cues in Sexual Deviation by Audio and Taped Descriptions." *Journal of Applied Behavior Analysis* 8: 1975.

——. "The Role of Fantasy in the Treatment of Sexual Deviation." *Archives of General Psychiatry* 30: 1974.

Annon, Jack S. *The Behavioral Treatment of Sexual Problems.* Honolulu: Kapioni Health Services. 1974.

Bjorksten, Oliver. "Premature Ejaculation; Success in Three Treatment Sessions." *Sexual Medicine Today* 2: October 1978.

Bibliography

Conrad, Andrée. "Sexual Practices in Ancient China." *Sexual Medicine Today* 2: October 1979.

Fisher, Charles, Raul Shiavi, H. Lear, A. Edwards, and D. M. Davis. "The Assessment of Nocturnal REM Erection in the Differential Diagnosis of Sexual Impotence." *Journal of Sex and Marital Therapy* 1: 1975.

Frank, Ellen, and Carol Anderson. "One Hundred Happily Married Couples Report on Their Sex Lives." A study conducted at the Western Psychiatric Institute and Clinic and the University of Pittsburgh School of Medicine. Reported in *Sexual Medicine Today* 2. Published later as "The Frequency of Sexual Dysfunction in Normal Couples." *The New England Journal of Medicine* 299: March 1978.

Gebhard, Paul H., and Alan B. Johnson. *The Kingsley Data: Marginal Tabulations of the 1938–1963 Interviews Conducted by the Institute for Sex Research.* Philadelphia: W. B. Saunders Company. 1979.

Hunter, John, F. R. S. *A Treatise on the Venereal Disease.* London: 1786. First American edition, Philadelphia: J. Webster. 1818.

LoPicolo, Joseph and Leslie. *Becoming Orgasmic: A Sexual Growth Program for Women.* Englewood Cliffs, New Jersey: Prentice-Hall, 1976.

LoPicolo, Leslie. "Low Sexual Desire." *Principles and Practice of Sex Therapy.* Leiblum, Sandra R., and Lawrence A. Pervin, editors. New York: The Guilford Press. 1980.

Marshall, William, and K. Lippens. "The Clinical Value of Boredom: A Procedure for Reducing Inappropriate Sexual Interests." *Journal of Nervous and Mental Diseases* 165: 1977.

Masters, William, and Virginia Johnson. *Human Sexual Inadequacy.* Boston: Little Brown & Co. 1970.

Semans, James H. "Premature Ejaculation: A New Approach." *Southern Medical Journal* 49: 1956.

Tuthill, J. F. "Impotence." *The Lancet.* January 15, 1955.

Virag, R. and H., L. Lajmgte, and D. Frydman. "A New Device to Measure the Rigidity of the Penis—Experimental & Clinical Evaluations." Paper read at 1st International Symposium on Impotence and Diabetes Mellitus. Panum Institute, University of Copenhagen, Denmark. August 1982.

Wagner, Gorm, and Richard Green. *Impotence.* New York: Plenum Press. 1981.

Weiss, Howard D. "The Physiology of Human Penile Erections." *Annals of Internal Medicine* 76: 1972.

INDEX

Abel, Gene G., 83*n*
Abel Scale of physical impotence, 83
Accessories, eroticism and, 44
Annon, Jack, 188
Annon's method of ejaculation control,
    188
Anxiety
    and erection loss, 85–87 (*see also* Erec-
        tion)
    impotence from, 82
    removal of, as cure for
        impotence, 90–93 (*see also* Behavio-
            ral impotence)
Arms and hands touching
    in cure for behavioral impotence, 106
    in Ten-Day Plan, 37–40
Arousal
    and ejaculation, 179, 180
    ejaculation control and lowering, 187,
        190, 193, 196–97, 199
    erections, lubrication, and orgasms fol-
        lowing, 27–29
    and erections past age of forty, 88–89
    and failing to restore erections, and fe-
        male erection, 134
    insufficient, as cause of impotence, 72
    as key to erection, 102–3
    law of, 208
    low, and loss of erection, 80–81
    lubrication and, 27–29, 133–36, 140
    as necessary for female orgasm, 154–55
    prolonged, after penetration, and prema-
        ture ejaculation, 182
    prolonged, before penetration, and pre-
        mature ejaculation, 182–83

seven actions to build female, 153
    as step to female orgasm, 146
    See also Desire
Autonomic nervous system
    erections controlled by, 78
    eroticism and, 28
    and lubrication, 134

Babies
    sex as making, 26–27
    See also Reproductive sex
Behavioral impotence, 82, 85–126
    breaking partial-erection habit to cure,
        117–19
    choosing worst kind of lovers to cure,
        96–101
    compulsive repetition as cure for, 95
    and dangers of "normal" sex, 119–21
    and failing to restore erections, 93
    and fear of expressing inner thoughts,
        107–10
    first and easiest cure for, 90–93
    five mistakes in seeking to cure self of,
        94–95
    and giving up best orgasm, 111–13
    and losing erection in front of a woman,
        121–22
    profile of impotent man, 87–88
    prostitute as cure for, 97–98
    as psychological attachment for mother,
        100–1
    reasons for maintaining, 104–5
    and right woman, 94
    rod-and-piston approach to, 94–95
    sex object and, 96–97

Behavioral impotence (*Cont.*)
  sex therapy and, 85
  staying away from women as cure for, 95
  touch and, 61, 73–74, 77, 84, 102, 105, 106
  of women, 145–46
  women's behavior aggravating, 98–100
  wrong assumptions about, 85
Biological impotence, *see* Physical impotence
Biological patterns, establishing, of ejaculation, 180–81 (*see also* Ejaculation)
Blood-flow
  and female erections, 133–34
  and long separation from lover, 89
  male erection and, 80–82
Bodies
  discovering new, of familiar lover, 32–33
  female orgasm and feeling own erotic, 152–53 (*see also* Female orgasm)
  need for change among erotic, 23–25 (*see also* Desire)
  new, 23, 24
  touch of whole, 102, 104, 105 (*see also* Touch)
  See also Ten-Day Plan
Body touching in Ten-Day Plan, 45–46

Chinese control of ejaculation, 185–87
Clitoris
  blood flow and erection of, 133–34
  as equivalent of penis, 137–38, 168, 170
  helping lover explore, female orgasm and, 167–70
  measuring erection of, during sleep, 146
  See also Vagina
Compulsive repetition as cure for behavioral impotence, 95

Desire, 17–54
  disappointment at losing, 20
  discovering needs in, building to orgasm, 162–63 (*see also* Orgasm)
  and erotic body's need for change, 23–25
  fulfilled, 17–18
  impotence caused by lack of, 62 (*see also* Arousal)
  justifying loss of, 25–26
  killing, 55–61
  as learned, 57
  losing, for lover's behavior, 30–31
  loss of, 18–20
  as in mind of lover, 59
  new-lover solution to lost, 31–33
  repetition destroying, 22

social inhibition of, and learning of, 57–58
  wrong beliefs about, 21–23
  See also Ten-Day Plan; Touch

Ejaculation
  developing quick, 177–78
  establishing biological pattern of, 180–81
  on her breasts, 53–54
  moment of inevitability of, 179–80
  premature, *see* Premature ejaculation
  timing of, 179
Ejaculation control
  achieved, 206–7
  Annon's method of, 188
  arousal and, 187, 190, 193, 196–97, 199
  Chinese method of, 185–87
  foreplay mastery for, 186, 188, 192, 207
  by frequent ejaculation, 187, 189, 193, 207
  how lover helps in, 204
  last moment crises in, 204–5
  and orgasmic woman, 186–88, 192, 207
  pitfalls of learning too fast, 201–2
  Semans's method of, 188–89
  sequential-thinking handicap to, 202–3
  stop-start (squeeze) method of, 187–93, 199–203, 207
Embarrassment of impotence, 71–73
Erection
  anxiety over loss of, 85–87 (*see also* Anxiety)
  becoming excellent lover without using, 102–4
  behavioral impotence and, *see* Behavioral impotence
  blood-flow and loss of, 80–82
  difficulty with maintaining, among happy men, 12–14
  fear of loss of, and premature ejaculation, 182
  five steps to, 102–3
  of impotent men, 77–78 (*see also* Impotence)
  losing, in front of a woman, 121–22
  loss of, in every man, 79–82
  as lying signal to desire, 44
  measuring female sleep, 146
  measuring male sleep, 84
  mistake of trying to keep, 122–25
  past age of forty, 88–90
  penetration and fear of loss of, 123–25
  temporary loss of, and behavioral impotence, 85–86 (*see also* Behavioral impotence)

of women, 133–34
wrong belief about masculinity and, 82
See also Arousal; Ejaculation; Ejaculation
control
Erotic delights, law of, 208, 209
Erotic success
as responsibility of lover, 102
See also Bodies; Desire

Female impotence, distinguishing between
physical and biological causes of,
145–46
Female orgasm, 127–73
achieving, 157
best, 138–39
better, 136–37
and choosing worst possible lover,
159–62
discovering female needs building to,
162–63
easy, 136
experiences inhibiting or promoting,
141–45, 147, 148
and fear of letting go, 156
first step to, 150–51
five steps to, 146–47
frigidity and, 130
and "his body for her," 172
lover's help in, 158–59
lubrication and having, *see* Lubrication
making love and failure to reach, 127–28
multiple and longer-lasting, 140
no-responsibility circle of failure in, 149
as problem of happy women, 12–14
reactive worries to lack of, 153–55
and reasons for remaining underaroused,
147
seven actions to build toward, 153
and thinking own erotic thoughts and
feeling own erotic body, 152–53
and trust, 128–33, 161, 165, 172–73
as up to the man, 132
and vibrators, 155–56
Fights, picking, to conceal loss of erection,
80
Foreplay mastery
to ejaculation control, 188, 192, 207
See also Desire
Forty (age), erections past, 88–89
Frank, Ellen, 12
Freud, Sigmund, 138–39
Frigidity
as obsolete term, 130
See also Female impotence; Female orgasm

George III (King of England), 91–93

Hands-on-hands learning, 42–43
Head and body touching in cure for behav-
ioral impotence, 106
Hite Report, The, 170
Hugging, stopping, to conceal loss of erec-
tion, 80
Hunter, John, 90–92

Impotence, 12, 13, 71–126
behavioral, 74–76, 82 (*see also* Behavioral
impotence)
case illustrating, 74–75
cause of, 61–62, 72, 83
concealing, 71–73
female, 145–46 (*see also* Female orgasm)
physical, *see* Physical impotence
questions to learn severity of, 76–77
secret desires and, 73–74
and unreasonable expectations, 81–82

Johnson, Virginia, 170, 184, 189–91
Johnson and Masters (squeeze) method,
187–93, 199–203, 207
Jokes, lowering arousal with, 63–64

Kinsey, Alfred, 12
Kissing, stopping, to conceal loss of erection, 80

Labeling
of relationship as sexual, to rescue desire,
68–69
of touch as nonsexual, to kill desire,
63–64
Language
nonsexual labels in, 64
See also Speech
Legs and feet touching
in cure for behavioral impotence, 106
in Ten-Day Plan, 43–45
Lover's Plan, *see* Ten-Day Plan
Lubrication
arousal and, 27–29, 133–36, 140
and female impotence, 145

Male impotence, *see* Behavioral impotence;
Impotence; Physical impotence
Male orgasm
behavioral impotence and goal of, 105
giving up best, 111–13
as incentive to reproduce, 29
infrequency of, as cause of premature
ejaculation, 181–82
See also Erection

Masters, William, 170, 184, 189–91
Motels, erotic, 99
Mothers
  and behavioral impotence, 100–1
  and female orgasm, 141–43, 147, 148
  impotence and, 75–76
  and trust between lovers, 129, 130

New lover as solution to lost desire for old
    lover, 31–33

Orgasm
  behavioral impotence and giving up best,
    111–13
  erections, lubrication, and, following
    arousal, 27–29
  See also Female orgasm; Male orgasm
Orgasmic women, ejaculation control and,
    186–88, 192, 207

Partial-erection habit, 117–19
Penis
  as equivalent of clitoris, 137–38, 168, 170
  vagina as not equivalent to, 136–38
Penis touching
  in cure for behavioral impotence, 106,
    110–11, 113–16
  impotence and, 73–74
  and sensitive spot, 51–52
  in Ten-Day Plan, 47–49
Penis-in-the-vagina intercourse
  behavioral impotence and, 106, 107,
    119–21
  and clitoris, 136
  and impotence, 102
  orgasm reinforced by, 29
  and premature ejaculation, 182
  prolonged arousal after penetration and
    premature ejaculation, 182
  prolonged arousal before penetration and
    premature ejaculation, 182–83
  in Ten-Day Plan, 33, 34
    touches, positions, and moments
      during, 49–51
Physical impotence, 74–76, 82–85
  Abel Scale to gauge, 83
  measuring male natural sleep erections
    and, 84
  vital steps before surgery for, 84–85
  of women, 145–46
Premature ejaculation, 175–207
  as any ejaculation before wanting to, 191
  as biological success, 190
  causes and situations in, 181–84
  change in latency to ejaculation and, 177

choosing worst kind of lover to deal
    with, 192–93
  circle of failure in, 195
  cure for, 185–91
  effect of establishing pattern of, 191
  experiences promoting, 176–77
  facts of, and how to stop, 178
  mistakes in seeking self cure for, 194–95
  orgasm and, *see* Male orgasm
  as problem of happy men, 12
  rejection of her rejection and, 197–99
Pregnancy, sex and fear of, 27
Prostitutes as cure for behavioral impo-
    tence, 97–98

Rejection
  of lover before touching, to kill desire,
    66–67
  of lover's rejection, 67–68
  premature ejaculation and, 197–99
Repetition, destroying desire through, 22
Reproductive sex
  eroticism confused with, 26–27
  as natural, 28–29
  replacing erotic sex, 29–30
Rod-and-piston approach to behavioral im-
    potence, 94–95
Rules regulating times for sex to conceal
    loss of erection, 80

Secrets of sex, 11–12
Self-cure
  mistakes in seeking, for behavioral impo-
    tence, 94–95
  mistakes in seeking, for premature ejacu-
    lation, 193–94
Semans, James, 184, 188–89, 204
Semans's method of ejaculation control,
    188–89
Separation and loss of erection, 89
Sex object, behavioral impotence and,
    96–97
Sexual success
  laws of, 208–9
  See also Desire
Social control, impotence and, 87
Social inhibition of desire, 57–58
Speech
  avoiding explanatory, to kill desire, 64
  impotence and fear of expressing inner
    thoughts in, 107–10
  use of, to learn, 40–41
Squeeze method of ejaculation control,
    187–93, 199–203, 207

Stop-start method of ejaculation control,
    187–93, 199–203, 207
Surgery
    as cause of female impotence, 146
    to move clitoris, 138
    steps before, for physical impotence,
        84–85
Surroundings, sex and new, 24–25

Ten-Day Plan (Ten Days to Erotic Discov-
    ery), 33–54
    for behavioral impotence, 105–7
    beyond his erection to her desire, 37–41
    day 1, 37–38
    day 2, 39–40
    day 3, 43
    day 4, 43–44
    day 5, 45
    day 6, 45–46
    day 7, 46–47
    day 8, 47–49
    day 9, 49
    day 10, 49
    following, before possible surgery for
        physical impotence, 84
    outline of, 33–36
    time to rediscover desire in, 36–37
Thoughts
    behavioral impotence and fear of express-
        ing inner, 107–10
    new, 24
    See also Desire; Speech
Time, taking, to discover desire, 36–37
Touch
    avoiding, to kill desire, 63
    and behavioral impotence, 61, 73–74, 77,
        84, 102, 105, 106
    belief in, to rescue desire, 70
    at best times, to rescue desire, 68

changing, to levels of desire, 49–51
convincing lover of uselessness of, to kill
    desire, 65
and details of desire, to rescue desire, 69,
    70
developing, and female orgasm, 163–67
to find other's desire, 37–41
as first step to female orgasm, 150–51
hands-on-hands, to learn, 42–43
her learning to, 39–40
his learning to, 37–38
and impotent man's fear of speaking his
    thoughts, 107–10
labeled as nonsexual, to kill desire, 63–64
law of, 208
and loss of erection, 86–87
new, 23, 24
reasons not to permit, 148
in rediscovery of lover's body, 33–36
rejection of lover before, to kill desire,
    66–67
speech to learn right, 40–41
as step to female orgasm, 147
of whole body, 102, 104, 105
Trust, 128–33, 161, 165, 172–73

Vagina
    exploring, 169–71
    impotence and fear of, 75–76
    not equivalent of penis, 136–38
    See also Clitoris; Female orgasm; Lubrica-
        tion; Penis-in-the-vagina intercourse
Vagina touching
    behavioral impotence and, 106, 113–15
    in Ten-Day Plan, 46–47
Vaginal infections, 146
Vibrators, 155–56

Water, sex in, 53